The legitimacy of quality assurance in higher education: the role of public authorities and institutions

Edited by Luc Weber and Katia Dolgova-Dreyer

Sjur Bergan (Series editor)

Council of Europe Publishing

Cover design: Graphic Design Studio, Council of Europe
Layout: Desktop Publishing Unit, Council of Europe

Council of Europe Publishing
F-67075 Strasbourg Cedex
http://book.coe.int

ISBN 978-92-871-6237-3
© Council of Europe, November 2007

Printed at the Council of Europe

Contents

The legitimacy of quality assurance

Appendix

Preface

Gabriele Mazza
Director of School, Out-of-school and Higher Education

I am proud to present herewith the ninth volume in the Council of Europe Higher Education Series, which was launched in December 2004. We give high priority to this series, as we strongly believe that there is a need for the Council of Europe to address topical and highly relevant issues of higher education in a format which is accessible not only to higher education professionals but also to all those interested in higher education, and who believe in the importance of higher education to modern society. The values of the European university heritage are also those of the Council of Europe.

This book is no exception. The theme of quality in higher education is one that we all instinctively understand the importance of, and one to which public authorities attach great importance. Nobody will deny that higher education should be of good quality. But why is it now becoming more important than ever, why is this a topic that keeps getting more and more attention? On the other hand, what are the possible disadvantages of the current emphasis on quality assurance? Is there a risk that by emphasising external quality assurance so strongly, we could in fact devise systems and procedures that will hamper rather than further the development of good quality? In this book you will find thoughts and reflections on the subject of the quality of higher education and public responsibility for it which provide answers to these questions.

I would like to draw your attention to one basic, but important consideration: the well-being and development of societies in the long-term perspective are becoming less and less dependent on mineral resources and production of material goods, and are more and more built on the "intangibles" – knowledge and know-how, understanding and the ability to transform knowledge to action. Hence, the more and better educated people society can have today, the better off it is going to be tomorrow. In a way, it is no longer the private sector that "feeds" the public sector, but the public sector by "producing" well-educated citizens contributes to generating future prosperity for society as well as for individual citizens. Thus, the good quality of higher education becomes a key element when building sustainable democratic societies.

I would like to thank the editors, Luc Weber and Katia Dolgova-Dreyer, as well as all the contributors for their excellent work on this new volume in our Higher Education Series. This book is very timely, as it comes at the moment when the ministers of education of the Bologna process identify new challenges at their meeting in London, on our way to establishing the European Higher Education Area.

A word from the series editor

Sjur Bergan

With the book you are about to read, the Council of Europe Higher Education Series addresses an issue that is among the most topical in the higher education debate today: quality assurance. It is an issue that it was entirely natural to take up in a series that aims to provide policy makers, practitioners, higher education specialists and general readers with an overview of the major topics in higher education.

However, there is also a danger in addressing quality assurance, precisely because so much has already been written about the topic. Marketing specialists may describe this particular challenge in terms of market saturation, whereas academics may phrase it in terms of breaking new ground in an area that has already been well studied.

Contributing new ideas to a topic, however, also requires looking at the context in which the topic is considered. This is, we hope, where this book will take a new approach. By considering quality assurance from the triple perspective of public responsibility, governance and legitimacy, this publication seeks to draw on the work of two previous Council of Europe fora – as well as two publications in the Higher Education Series – and also on the role of the Council of Europe as a pan-European organisation in which ideas can be discussed and placed into their proper context. This publication does not seek to impose a given model, but it does explore a good number of issues related to quality assurance as well as offering some examples of how the main principles of quality assurance, outlined in the standards and guidelines adopted by European ministers of education at the ministerial meeting of the Bologna Process held in Bergen in 2005, may be implemented in different countries and circumstances.

Another important point to make – and one that is being made by several contributors to this book – is that quality assurance is not just a matter of checking *post facto* whether the desired quality is there, and then taking corrective action if it is not. Put simply, if we believe quality assurance is important, we must also believe that it is important to ensure there is quality in the first place. Put in slightly less simplistic terms, there can be no quality assurance without quality development. Put in more technical terms that may become more meaningful once the book has been read, external quality assurance is a complement to internal quality assurance and development. While quality assurance may be the political catch word and make the front page in the education press, quality development is the daily and ongoing concern of staff and students as well as of policy makers at institutions and in ministries. It is where quality development is not a prime concern of practitioners and policy makers that quality assurance takes on a key importance and may indeed call for corrective action.

This volume of the Council of Europe Higher Education Series, then, sets out to explore a well-studied topic from new angles, to contribute to as well as supplement the current policy debate in Europe. This book draws on the contributions of prominent

European policy makers, some of whom may rightly be considered quality assurance specialists and others who, while they are well acquainted with the issues of quality assurance, consider them in the light of their expertise in and experience from other areas of higher education policies. All of them weigh substantially in the European debate, and I would like to thank them for their contribution to the Higher Education Series. I would also like to put on record my gratitude to the editors of this volume. Luc Weber is an experienced policy maker, researcher and writer on whose expertise we have been able to draw both for previous volumes in the Higher Education Series and more broadly in the Council of Europe's higher education programme, currently also as Chair of our Steering Committee for Higher Education and Research (CDESR). My Council of Europe colleague Katia Dolgova-Dreyer is newer to the field and has recently taken over as Secretary to the CDESR. This publication marks her debut as an editor.

May this combination of experience and freshness symbolise what we have tried to do with this book: take a central topic, on which much ink has already been spilled, look at it from new angles and put together a collection of articles that will hopefully make for stimulating reading and give rise to continued debate.

A word from the editors

Luc Weber and Katia Dolgova-Dreyer

Higher education and research are changing radically in Europe today. The outstanding feature is undoubtedly the Bologna process (with ministerial meetings in 1999, 2001, 2003 and 2005 as well as a meeting of four ministers at the Sorbonne in 1998), a joint effort by 45 European countries to create a European Higher Education Area, facilitating student mobility and turning European diversity into a genuine asset. People familiar with the project know that it rests upon 10 pillars, the two best known being the division of university studies into three cycles, bachelor's, master's and doctorate, and the use of a uniform system of credits (European Credit Transfer System – ECTS) to measure students'progress. A third pillar is becoming increasingly important at present: the focus on the quality of institutions of higher education thanks to the generalisation of quality assurance or accreditation. The application of the Council of Europe/UNESCO Recognition Convention (1997) is also relevant here.

But the upheavals affecting higher education and research in Europe do not stop there – far from it. Globalisation and the dazzling progress of science and technology are having two decisive effects:

- an increasingly competitive climate, which primarily affects businesses and individuals, but is now impacting on universities too: there is growing competition between traditional universities, which themselves face a growing challenge from new-style institutions: remote-study and/or transborder universities, private for-profit and corporate universities;
- in the face of fierce competition from emergent economies, such as those of China and India, which are able to produce at very low cost, and also, thanks to improved education, break new ground, the developed countries must – if they want to preserve their privileged living standards – fully invest in the knowledge society. Indeed, this situation already exists in Europe itself, as a result of modernisation in central and eastern European countries. The expansion of the European Union from 15 member states in early 2004 to 27 today is a clear indication of the changes, and of the challenges. This competition represents a major challenge for the governance and leadership of institutions of higher education, and particularly universities. To meet it, and contribute effectively to the knowledge society through their teaching and research, universities must be largely autonomous from the state and private sponsors – which implies, conversely, that they must be effectively governed and led, and themselves pay scrupulous attention to the quality of the services they provide.

In other words, radical change, the Bologna Process and the new competitive climate have now made the concept of quality – in the sense of quality assurance or better quality culture or quality improvement – which has long been omnipresent in the field of research, one of the key themes in the present debate on higher education policy.

Its belated arrival on the scene is surprising, since quality has long been regarded as a vital concept in all systems for the exchange of goods or services. Market systems (essentially private sector) and non-market systems (essentially public sector) both function better when the quality of goods, services and production factors is promoted by effective penalties and rewards. In the market system, penalties and rewards are impersonal, market-determined and essentially reflected in sales. In the public sector, where buying and selling are not generally part of the picture, they are indirect, and chiefly reflected in political support. Looking at this question in connection with higher education is particularly interesting since, although nearly all higher education institutions and universities are public institutions, a private sector has been emerging in the last fifteen years or so, chiefly in the countries of central and eastern Europe.

The co-existence of a public and a private system raises a whole series of questions relating to public responsibility and governance, both of the system and of institutions. This is why the Council of Europe's Steering Committee for Higher Education and Research (CDESR) organised two fora and published two books discussing and summarising the present position on these two issues, that is, a forum on "Public responsibility" in autumn 2004 (Weber and Bergan) and another on "Governance" in autumn 2005 (Kohler and Huber). This is also why, since quality assurance is becoming a key element in public responsibility and governance, it organised a third forum on "The legitimacy of quality assurance in higher education".

This book is a collection of the most relevant contributions to this forum. It is organised in three main parts. The first of these sets the scene by outlining approaches to and rationales for quality assurance.

Luc Weber, as co-editor of this book, gives an overview of the development of quality assurance in Europe. He underlines that quality assurance is still a relatively recent phenomenon, but that the theory and practice of quality assurance have now reached a stage of maturity that is beyond that of adolescence, and that it would have been difficult to predict had we looked at quality assurance even ten years ago. It is, accidentally, a measure of developments in this area that in 1996–97 it proved impossible to include binding provisions on quality assurance in the Council of Europe/UNESCO Recognition Convention because, at the time, there was still disagreement between potential signatories on whether a formal system for quality assurance was needed. Now, ten years later, the discussion is no longer on whether a quality assurance system is needed, but on what this system should be like. We would also argue that a party to the convention which did not make reference to the outcomes of its external quality assurance when giving an overview of the institutions that make up its higher education system would not be fulfilling its obligations under the convention (Council of Europe/UNESCO).

Alberto Amaral follows up this initial article by examining the challenges public authorities and institutions face in a situation characterised by an increasing emphasis on market mechanisms. His reflections clearly link to those undertaken at the Council of Europe forum on the public responsibility for higher education and research (Weber and Bergan), and Amaral explores the roles, responsibilities and means at the disposal of these essentially non-market actors in a market-dominated situation.

The two following articles in this section look at specific aspects of quality assurance. From his perspective as the head of a national quality assurance agency, Ossi V. Lindqvist explores the role of agencies not only in auditing quality but in fostering quality. The important point that quality is not only a question of control but even more of policies to foster development was made by all contributors, and it is taken up by Jürgen Kohler in the final article of this part of the book, where he looks at implications for the governance of institutions as well as of systems. In this way, Jürgen Kohler provides a direct link between the forum that led to this book and the previous forum on higher education governance (Kohler and Huber).

The second section places the quality assurance debate in the context of the European Higher Education Area, of which it has become a centrepiece. At their meeting in Bergen in May 2005, European ministers adopted standards and guidelines for quality assurance in the European Higher Education Area. In his article, Peter Williams, who played a key role in the elaboration of the standards and guidelines, outlines them and explores the way in which they may be implemented within each higher education system that makes up the Area.

The implementation of the standards and guidelines is further described by two articles that look at their effect and implementation in specific national contexts. In her article, Patricia Georgieva describes the situation of a country – Bulgaria – that has undergone an extensive transformation in the course of the past fifteen years or so. Ireland, which is the subject of Fergal Costello's article, has also undergone profound changes, but in a very different way from Bulgaria. In the Irish case, it is also interesting to note that the public authorities have entrusted the universities with a decisive role in quality assurance. In both cases, as in many other European countries, higher education is seen as essential to the future of society, and how best to ensure the quality of higher education is therefore no small matter.

In his article, Andrejs Rauhvargers discusses the relationship between quality assurance and the recognition of qualifications. Quality assurance assesses the overall quality of an institution or, in some cases, of a study programme, whereas the purpose of recognition is to assess the achievement of an individual. Therefore, recognition specialists need to make use of the outcomes of quality assurance, and quality assurance specialists need to formulate their conclusions in such a way as to be useful to recognition specialists. Quality assurance will greatly facilitate recognition, but recognition does not follow automatically from quality assurance. This is an aspect of the uses of the outcomes of quality assurance, which is the subject of Norman Sharp's contribution as the final article in this second section.

In the third section, Lewis Purser, who was General Rapporteur of the forum, brings the different threads together in a consideration of the legitimacy of quality assurance.

In his article, Lewis Purser places special emphasis on the role of public authorities and institutions, and his considerations lead naturally to the set of recommendations that were adopted by the forum and that are reproduced as the final part of this third section.

Much has been written about quality assurance in higher education over the past decade or more, and much will undoubtedly be written in the coming decade. We hope the present book will be a valuable addition to the quality assurance literature, both by the quality of the articles and by the focus of this book on the triangle of public responsibility, governance and legitimacy. May this book also contribute to enhance an understanding that while quality assurance is essential to the development of the European Higher Education Area and to the position of European higher education in a global context, mechanisms of audit cannot substitute the most essential factor of all: the need for public authorities, institutions and individual students and staff to continually strive for the highest possible quality in teaching, learning and research. Quality assurance makes no sense except as the corollary to quality development and a quality culture.

We cannot end without thanking those who contributed to making the conference and this publication possible. The authors and presenters, as will become clear through the reading of this book, provided valuable insight, and the variety of their perspectives help reflect the diversity that is a hallmark of Europe as well as the unity that brings us together in a European Higher Education Area. The members of the Bureau of the Steering Committee for Higher Education and Research not only took the initiative to organise this conference but also provided valuable ideas as work on it progressed. We would in particular like to thank Radu Damian, Jürgen Kohler and Virgílio Meira Soares for their contributions. At the Council of Europe, Sophie Ashmore, Can Kaftancı and Mireille Wendling contributed greatly to organising the conference. The European University Association, represented by Andrée Sursock, and ENQA – the European Association for Quality Assurance in Higher Education – represented by Stefanie Hofmann, were invaluable partners in organising the conference and from their different perspective were instrumental in making sure that the conference and the book covered the different aspects and angles of quality assurance.

Stefanie Hofmann passed away unexpectedly in July 2006, some two months before the conference she had put so much effort into organising.

References

Bergen communiqué (2005), www.bologna-bergen2005.no/Docs/00-Main_doc/050520_Bergen_Communique.pdf

Berlin communiqué (2003) *Realising the European Higher Education Area*, www.bologna-bergen2005.no/Docs/00-Main_doc/030919Berlin_Communique.PDF

Bologna declaration (1999), www.bologna-bergen2005.no/Docs/00-Main_doc/990719BOLOGNA_DECLARATION.PDF

Council of Europe/UNESCO (1997) *Convention on the Recognition of Qualifications concerning Higher Education in the European Region*, Strasbourg/Paris

Kohler, J. and Huber, J. (eds) (2006) *Higher education governance between democratic culture, academic aspiration and market forces*, Council of Europe Higher Education Series No. 5, Strasbourg

Prague communiqué (2001), www.bologna-bergen2005.no/Docs/00-Main_doc/010519PRAGUE_COMMUNIQUE.PDF

Sorbonne Joint Declaration (1998), www.bologna-bergen2005.no/Docs/00-Main_doc/980525SORBONNE_DECLARATION.PDF

Weber, L. and Bergan, S. (eds) (2005) *The Public responsibility for higher education and research*, Council of Europe Higher Education Series No. 2, Strasbourg

Quality assurance:
approaches and rationales

Quality assurance in European higher education: from adolescence to maturity

Luc Weber

1. Preamble

On the background of the premises and environment described in the preface of this book, the objective of this paper is to contribute to the critical assessment of the progress made over the last quarter of a century in quality assurance – used here as a generic term – in higher education institutions and particularly in universities. The point of view will be that of an academic who has led a research university, and who has had the privilege over the last decade to evaluate some 20 universities and faculties within different frameworks and according to different methodologies, although mainly those of the "Institutional evaluation programme" of the European University Association (EUA).

This contribution shall in a first part (2.) try to indicate why quality assurance is so important in higher education today. This question will be considered from a double angle: first, from the standpoint of public authorities (2.1) and second, from the standpoint of institutions of higher education, in particular research universities (2.2). The second part (3.) will try to define how public authorities and institutions can best meet this shared responsibility. This will lead us to remind actors of what a university really is (3.1), to affirm that quality assurance is still in an adolescent phase (3.2) and to discuss the pros and cons of the most important choices which have to be made while searching for the best methodology of quality assurance (3.3). The chapter will then conclude (4.) in the light of what has been identified before, by considering the types of quality assurance which are most likely to help improve the quality of higher education, and so bring it to maturity.

2. Why?

2.1. Public responsibility

The forum organised by the Steering Committee for Higher Education and Research (CDESR) in autumn 2004 on Public Responsibility for Higher Education and Research (Weber and Bergan, 2005) unequivocally confirmed the responsibility of the state for higher education and research. There are at least two reasons for this:

- Higher education extensively benefits the whole community, including people who have not themselves been to university. It is the key element in the knowledge society, and an increasingly important factor of economic development.

Moreover, it contributes to the social and cultural enrichment, and the cohesion and sustainability,[1] of nations and the world at large.

- Governments must ensure, in accordance with the United Nations Declaration of Human Rights, that all those who are capable of benefiting from higher education have access to it (United Nations, 1948, UNESCO, 1998). They must eliminate barriers to access which are rooted in discrimination on grounds of gender, skin colour, religion, or connected with financial capacity. They must also remedy the lack of information on the benefits of higher education suffered by groups who have previously had no access to it. In other words, they are expected, not only to provide higher education, but also to finance and produce it partly or wholly.

Governments should pay attention to the quality of higher education and research for at least three reasons:

- because they spend large sums on it;
- because there is no automatic and effective system of penalties and rewards in the public sector;
- because they need to join in the communal effort to establish the European Higher Education and Research Area.

These were the considerations which led the ministers of education involved in the Bologna Process to insist, at their meetings in Prague (2001), Berlin (2003) and Bergen (2005) and in the associated communiqués, on the vital need for quality assurance in European universities.

In other words, no one denies that governments are responsible for the quality of the institutions of higher education which they supervise. But does that responsibility stop there, or extend to other institutions too? A look at the higher education offered in various parts of the world makes it clear that government involvement is not a *sine qua non*: nearly everywhere, except – for the moment – in western Europe, there is an enormous increase in the number of private, for-profit institutions, which sell their services to students-consumers. In principle, the state puts no money into these private institutions – but does this mean that it can ignore what they do and how they do it? Opinions and practices differ from country to country, but governments are increasingly showing a desire to monitor the quality of these institutions too, chiefly for the purpose of protecting students-consumers. This is consistent with the economic wisdom which leads them to monitor and regulate other private activities; their aim is to guarantee healthy competition and ensure that the quality of services – not easily judged by non-specialists – is at least acceptable.

---

1. We mean by "sustainable" social system a system which respects and applies a whole series of social values, such as democracy, respect for human rights, legal settlement of conflicts, tolerance, and fair distribution of revenues and wealth, thus ensuring that the tensions inherent in any social system do not augment to a point where the system itself is endangered.

2.2. The need for quality in institutions of higher education

This reminder of governments'responsibility for quality assurance in higher education may suffice to justify quality assurance, but it still leaves a great deal unsaid. To understand the real issues and select the best methods, it is essential to realise that quality assurance is also vital for the institutions themselves. We may cite two arguments here:

- The first concerns the autonomy of institutions of higher education. Looking at the general history of universities and at the factors which determine their individual excellence, we can see that the best are nearly always those which enjoy considerable autonomy. It is this which allows them to adopt a proactive or entrepreneurial stance and escape a classic vicious circle, in which restrictions to autonomy, more upstream supervision, political micro-management and the multiform external (usually cyclical) pressures which affect numerous universities in continental Europe all combine to sap their dynamism and reduce their sense of internal responsibility. Instead of taking the initiative, they respond when prodded, which makes government feel that it needs to play a bigger part – and this inevitably puts the institutions even more on the defensive. In short, restrictions on the autonomy of universities – even those honestly intended for their own good – reduce their quality, instead of improving it.
- Most European universities are seriously short of funds, chiefly because the absolute increase in public funding falls a long way short of cushioning the financial impact of rising student numbers (in itself, a very positive development). This means that even more emphasis must be laid on direction and management of universities, the aim being to ensure that they respond as effectively as possible to the most pressing needs.

Having said that, we have to decide whether universities are sufficiently well governed and run to justify the autonomy they demand and meet the challenge of under-funding. University staff, and particularly academic staff, seem convinced at all events that the shared management system – in which they hold a dominant position, even though the participation of students and other groups is institutionalised – guarantees optimum quality of teaching and research. It is true that lengthy training and the stiff competition they face when appointed, and later when seeking research grants and getting papers published in leading journals, are serious guarantees of their ability and desire to operate effectively. Also relevant is the fact that universities can meet new requirements when appointing new staff. Nonetheless, although this very decentralised system allows universities to adjust to a constantly changing environment, the question remains: does it ensure that they adjust sufficiently? Here, doubt is allowed. For one thing, there are various factors which make adjustment hard, when people are left entirely to their own decisions (Weber, 2006a and b). For another, existing systems of university governance are rarely conducive to strategic decision-making, and the people in charge – even outstanding academics – are not always natural leaders or able to exercise genuine leadership. This being so, we can safely say that the quality of most institutions is lower than it could or should be.

There are two opposing viewpoints on this situation and its effects:

- Governments conclude – not unreasonably – that it is unacceptable, and feel obliged to intervene and compel universities to do better.
- Universities need to realise that, with competition increasing and resources declining, they stand to gain by taking themselves in hand and improving their performance. They also need to realise that failure to do so may prompt government to step in and do it for them, using methods which they may regard as inappropriate, or even positively harmful. In other words, universities need to develop, in their own best interests, a genuine, pervasive culture of quality aiming at improvement. Moreover, the more autonomous an institution is of its supervising authority, the more it needs a rigorous quality assurance system – and this, we should remember, depends on sound governance, leadership and management.

3. How?

The points we have made, and the arguments we have used, in the first part make it clear that quality assurance – a generic term – is a necessity. First of all, it is an essential task for government, given the importance of higher education for society, the climate of confidence required by the Bologna Process and the need to regulate private provision. Secondly, it is directly in the interest of higher education institutions themselves, which have everything to gain by using their funds to optimum effect, and are usually unable – because of their lack of autonomy and usually poor governance – to act in the manner which would benefit them most. Having clearly shown that quality assurance in higher education institutions is necessary, from the standpoint of public responsibility and of university governance, we must now consider what we can do to ensure that the efforts made along these lines produce real improvements, and to minimise their harmful side effects. This is a delicate question and to answer it, we need a sound grasp of what an institution of higher education, and particularly a university, is.

3.1. The special character of higher education institutions

Higher education institutions, and particularly universities, are unique human institutions, if only because they are among our oldest, perhaps even the oldest types of institution. They are chiefly special in what they do, and in their ways of doing it. Universities in particular:

- are repositories of human knowledge, and have the task of transmitting the most useful and/or recent knowledge to their students and, even more, teaching them to learn, that is, encouraging them to stay curious and equipping them to keep track of future developments in their own fields;
- are places where research generates new knowledge and by sharing it, help to ensure that it benefits society. They also have a near-monopoly on the training of young researchers;

- use their knowledge and methods to benefit society by subjecting its problems to fully independent and scientific scrutiny and disseminating human knowledge as broadly as possible.

In other words, institutions of higher education and universities have a major responsibility to the communities and public organisations which fund their teaching and research, the individuals and firms which support them directly, and the students who follow their courses. Their debt to all these groups is considerable, and they have a duty to provide high-quality teaching and do high-quality research, and also serve the community.

The special character of higher education institutions can be brought out even more clearly by looking at the nature of the services they provide. It hardly needs saying that these have little in common with the services provided by other public or semi-public bodies which are subject to regular assessment, for example public transport companies.

On the teaching side, the vast amount of knowledge – even in limited fields – obliges them to strike a balance between transmitting "factual" or "pre-digested" knowledge, training people to learn, and transmitting concepts and methods which go a long way beyond factual or vocational knowledge. The knowledge acquired by the time students graduate is not easily measured, since the quality of an education is largely determined by the individual's learning capacity, and appears in what he/she does with it in the early years of a subsequent career. In other words, if an institution is assessed on the knowledge acquired by students at a given point in their studies, the result will partly depend also on factors over which it has little control.

Assessment of research faces similar difficulties. Of course, it seems easy to measure the effectiveness of a research project by comparing its results with those expected and/or considering the impact of the publications it generates. But how do we assess an ambitious project which produces results totally different from those expected? Also important is a project's innovative character – a longer-term thing, and so far harder to measure. And how can we assess research done by philosophers, literary theorists or mathematicians, who spend months reading and thinking, need no extra funding, and finally set out their conclusions in sometimes very short publications?

3.2. Quality assurance in the adolescent phase

Although the first quality assurance initiatives were taken more than twenty years ago, when quality agencies were established in countries like the Netherlands, the United Kingdom and France, we have no hesitation in saying that quality assurance in higher education is still at the adolescent stage. One proof of this is the broad range of terms still applied to specific approaches, of which the following, non-exhaustive list (Vlasceanu et al., 2004) gives a fair sample: accreditation, quality assessment, quality audit, quality assurance, licensing, certification, ranking, classification (Carnegie), benchmarking, quality control, culture of quality, descriptors, "summative" and "formative" assessment, quality evaluation, evaluation by students, standardisation, total quality management, qualification, recognition, (quality) review, standards, ISO standards, and so on. Moreover, the procedures associated with them apply to institutions, curricula, sub-divisions (faculties, departments), subject areas, courses, research projects – and the list continues.

Taken overall in Europe, this situation can well be termed chaotic, and its effects are negative, if not seriously harmful.

- **It does not work.** In accreditation systems, experience shows that only a very small minority of institutions or courses fail to get it, and when the system foresees an assessment, it usually has little effect, since its conclusions are not followed up by corrective measures.
- **The cost–benefit ratio is unsatisfactory.** Quality assurance is invariably costly, particularly when it is based on a self-assessment report by the institution and inspection by experts. An institution which takes self-assessment seriously commits substantial resources (particularly working time) to it, and outside experts are expensive. And if the results of the exercise are useless to the institution, or the institution ignores them, the situation becomes completely unsatisfactory.
- **It encourages institutions to behave strategically and agencies to become bureaucratic.** Some types of evaluation procedures prompt institutions to behave strategically, highlighting their strengths and concealing their weaknesses, instead of facing up to the latter and working on them. As for the assessing agencies, their determination to be objective may lead them to adopt a bureaucratic stance, treating set procedures and predetermined criteria as more important than the actual assessment. Moreover, as with accreditation, where assessment ultimately sets out to penalise, unequal treatment is a danger, since the line between compliance and non-compliance with the criteria is a very thin one for institutions which are already at the bottom of the list. The ultimate danger is that the results may be arbitrary.
- **The spread of quality assurance and certain associated strategies are turning quality assurance itself into a business.** As methods become more ambitious and refined, so the number of experts they depend on increases, while those experts become less inclined to work for nothing, simply to help a sister institution. Quality assurance is in danger of becoming a full-scale business enterprise, with all the problems of independence which that inevitably entails.

As we see it, the fact that quality assurance has so far developed so chaotically reflects a lack of adequate research on its scientific and managerial foundations. Essentially, we have had a succession of spontaneous and usually political initiatives, launched in response to immediate pressures by authorities which do not always grasp the full complexity of the task. The result is a tendency to reinvent the wheel, that is, take no account of the experience of others and fail to allow for the very special features of institutions of higher education. This airy assumption that "it's quite simple really" explains why we have so many different terms and approaches. No surprise, then, that no one is really satisfied, and that countries are constantly reviewing their methods. But it is a surprise that "scientific" institutions can so totally forget to apply scientific methods to the formulation of quality assurance policies.

3.3. Strategic choices in quality assurance

In devising a national quality assurance system, a country has to choose from among a whole range of alternative solutions, and its choice determines the thinking behind the approach it adopts. We now mean to identify and discuss the main options.

3.3.1. "Formative" or "summative"?

Without necessarily differing much in their approach, quality assurance procedures can have vastly different aims. "Formative" procedures are chiefly designed to help institutions or activities to improve their performance. Here, the purpose of assessment is to help them to form a clearer picture of the things they do well, and the things they do less well – and take the necessary ameliorative action. This approach embodies the spirit which feeds into development of a genuine culture of quality, that is quality improvement.

"Summative" procedures lead to a decision which, in its simplest form, says whether or not a quality test – whatever its form – has been passed. Accreditation, registration or certification are examples.

Some people may think this distinction a minor one, but it leads the institutions concerned to adopt wholly different attitudes. An institution seeking accreditation will obviously use its best persuasive powers to show how good it is, or how well it satisfies the criteria; it will adopt a strategy of trying to conceal, or at least minimise, weaknesses of which it is aware. The situation with formative assessment is diametrically different. An institution which takes the exercise seriously, and is conscious of its responsibilities, has everything to gain from revealing both its weaknesses and strengths, that is, conducting a full-scale SWOT (strengths, weaknesses, opportunities, threats) analysis, while an institution seeking accreditation may well lose out by playing the truth game and putting all its cards on the table.

3.3.2. Stated aims or pre-determined standard criteria?

This second choice raises a problem similar to the first one. A procedure based on pre-determined standard criteria certainly has the advantage of providing a uniform basis of comparison for assessment of institutions, curricula, and so on. At first sight, this would seem to make for equal treatment. But to what extent can different institutions, curricula or sub-divisions be validly assessed on set criteria? Such assessment may be perfectly valid when the criteria are general and widely accepted, for example division of studies into three cycles, or use of the credit system in the Bologna process, but it becomes highly dubious when scientific content or educational method are the issue, since these are, by definition, non-standard and changing all the time. This is why the alternative approach – basing assessment on aims declared and pursued – is often better suited to higher education institutions. Fitness for purpose is, in other words, the focus. The apparent loss of rigour is offset by an approach which emphasises the institution's effort at self-criticism and the sound judgment of the experts who have to decide whether the things it is doing will allow it to achieve its goals. This new paradigm may seem less satisfactory to start with, but is rendered necessary by the inherent nature of the services which universities provide.

3.3.3. Qualitative or quantitative?

Measuring all the relevant criteria and rating quality as a percentage of a maximum, perfect score would seem the surest path to objective assessment. Obviously, this kind of rigour would be ideal – if it were possible. The problem here is that the realities of higher education are not easily reduced to figures. Of course, there are many data, such as student and graduate numbers, surfaces, funds, books, publications, which can indeed be measured, broken down into categories and sub-categories, and used to generate a whole series of arithmetical ratios which can then be used to gauge specific forms of efficiency and/or facilitate comparisons.

The real situation is more complex, however, and quantification of this kind can give a dangerous impression of accuracy. The main problem is that many of the things measured (the indicators) are not homogeneous or sufficiently relevant. For example, in measuring staff/student ratios, one would have to make distinctions based on subject area, level of study, duration of course, degree obtained and origins of students, and so on, and make appropriate distinctions for teaching staff as well. In the same way, better results at the end of the first year may be due to a lowering of standards – which may bump up the failure rate at the end of the second year. The fact is, using numerical data to compare institutions can easily lead to false conclusions.

To measure academic output, we need to consider the quality of publications or their impact, both immediate and longer-term. To assess the value of a library, simply counting the books is clearly not enough: we need to consider whether they are still useful, and whether they are easily accessible. Similarly, to assess the quality of a specific study course, it is not enough, for example, to look at the percentage of graduates who find jobs within six months – we must also consider the quality of those jobs, and see what graduates of five years' standing are doing today. The champions of quantitative assessment are obviously aware of these difficulties and are constantly refining their measurement procedures. With proper resources, this is perfectly possible in certain areas – but becomes very difficult once we try to establish an arithmetic ratio between two quantities (indicators) and use it to assess academic content, for example effectiveness of courses, or include the temporal dimension.

3.3.4. The institution or an agency?

The first quality assurance procedures were mainly the brainchild of governments, which set up quality agencies, usually attached to government departments, or simply launched ad hoc assessment schemes. Attention focused chiefly on individual institutions, academic output, curricula or the level in specific subject areas, and the aim was comparison or accreditation. Assessment was primarily external, and institutions themselves played only a minor part in the process. One consequence of this, which we have already mentioned, was that institutions bent over backwards to make the best impression and took little notice of the findings afterwards – unless, of course, they were denied accreditation.

This explains the current trend towards maximum involvement of the people responsible for institutions, curricula and so on. The subsidiarity principle – that decisions must be taken and implemented on the lowest level where their effectiveness is certain – is cited in support of this. Indeed, this was the attitude adopted by the Bologna Process ministers, when they declared in their Berlin communiqué (2003) that "consistent with the principle of institutional autonomy, the primary responsibility for quality assurance in higher education lies with each institution itself". The first stage of quality assurance should be entrusted to institutions, not only because developing a culture of quality is in their interest, but also because they are best equipped for the task. In practice, they should themselves assess quality of teaching, curricula, teaching and research units (faculties, departments, etc.) and administrative services (that is, student affairs, library and computer services, etc.) using the best method in each case. Courses should be assessed mainly by students, and curricula, teaching and research units, and administrative services be assessed via a three-stage procedure: self-assessment report, inspection and report by independent experts, and rigorous follow-up action on the conclusions.

Institutions and supervising authorities would be wrong to assume, however, that institutions themselves will necessarily make the best job of assessment. For this reason, quality assurance procedures carried out by institutions should themselves be assessed at regular intervals by national or international agencies, or agencies specialising in specific subject areas. The procedure itself would be very much the same: self-assessment report, inspection and report by experts, and follow-up action on the findings.

In systems of this kind, which follow the subsidiarity principle, institutions clearly cannot assess themselves; in principle, they should again be assessed by an external agency specialised in institutional or programme assessment. It is vital that assessment should not stop at internal quality procedures, but should also look at an institution's ability to change, that is, act on a strategic vision and on the conclusions of assessment.

Taking things to their logical conclusion, it is clear that these agencies must themselves be assessed, and probably accredited or approved. This is even more important when assessment is a commercial operation; for then the worst and the best may lie close together. If we are serious about a European Higher Education Area, then we must also accept a situation in which countries (not just small countries, where setting up national agencies is impractical) and institutions are willing to be assessed by foreign agencies. At their meeting in Bergen (2005), the ministers opted for a register of approved agencies. This question is discussed elsewhere in this book; we shall merely say that this is another political initiative which may be hard, if not impossible, to implement, and that there is a danger that many countries may not take decisions by the register to approve agencies seriously.

Obviously, governments have a duty to ensure that agencies monitor the procedures which institutions use to assess their own quality – and also assess institutions overall. It is also important that governments, governmental organisations, and associations of institutions of higher education and students should conclude a formal agreement on assessment and approval of these agencies.

3.3.5. Other questions

Obviously, there are other questions which need answering when quality assurance systems are being planned or adjusted at international, national or institutional level. Since space is at a premium and other contributors will be discussing them, we shall mention only four of them here. We need to:

- determine whether assessment findings affect institutions financially and, if so, how: do they reward quality or help institutions to make the necessary improvements? We have actually answered this question earlier: "formative" assessment, that is, assessment which has nothing to do with penalties, accreditation or funding, is the only kind which provides a basis for objective commitment to improvement. Having said that, growing competition also makes it essential to match funding to performance;
- guarantee the independence of assessment agencies, which must not be answerable to governments or universities, and ensure that the various viewpoints get an equal hearing. But is this really possible in a situation where agencies – since universities cannot afford to pay them – are funded almost totally by governments?
- guarantee the independence of experts. At first sight, finding independent experts might seem easy, but things may become more complicated once the question of payment for the very considerable work involved arises. Also, particularly in smaller countries, it may be very difficult to find experts who do not in some way know – or have even worked with – many of those whose work is being assessed. This is a strong argument in favour of bringing in foreign experts in a quality assessment exercise, but this is of course costly and may also give rise to problems of language;
- decide whether the assessment findings should be published. The aim of transparency suggests that they should be, but this inevitably leads experts to

phrase their conclusions far more "diplomatically", particularly when individuals are affected.

4. Conclusion – towards maturity

Obviously, the space available in this book does not allow us to cover all aspects of establishing a culture of quality at European, national and institutional level. We hope, however, that the points we have made on the legitimacy of quality assurance, and on the main choices which the very special character of institutions of higher education obliges us to make, will contribute to the development of more mature approaches. The need for a culture of quality in higher education is undeniable. It is rooted in governments' responsibility for higher education – a responsibility recently given a new dimension by the Sorbonne-Bologna process, which depends, among other things, on greater mutual trust between institutions of higher education in Europe. It is also rooted in the duty which every institution has to do its job as well as it can, better, to surpass themselves. This is particularly true of universities, which insist on having (and actually have) a large degree of autonomy, and regard that as essential to fulfilment of their task in a radically changing world. We should remember that, unlike the market, where penalties and rewards are automatic and effective, the public system has to use special instruments to reward good performers and penalise bad.

Twenty-five years of trying, not always successfully, to bring quality assurance into higher education and research have given us considerable experience, both positive and negative, and this helps us to clarify the picture. In this conclusion, we shall try to draw some practical lessons from our discussion of the methodological choices we face when planning quality assurance systems at institutional, national and international level.

Let us start by repeating that:

- the procedure should match the exceptional complexity of institutions of higher education and the services they provide;
- it should be more formative than punitive;
- it should be focused on the future, and particularly institutions' capacity for change;
- it should respect the subsidiarity principle;
- it should mobilise institutions and the various groups within them;
- its costs should be in line with the benefits it can reasonably be expected to provide;
- the experts appointed, either individually or within agencies, should be independent;
- the assessments done on one level should be monitored by a body on a higher level;
- stated aims, and not pre-determined standard criteria, should be the basis of assessment;
- appraisal by experts should be preferred to quantitative measurement, while recognising that carefully formulated indicators are useful.

These criteria are considered important for effective quality assurance. They were the basis of the approach adopted over ten years ago by the European Rectors' Conference (CRE), which today constitutes the beacon programme of the recently created European University Association (EUA) (successor to the CRE and to the European Union Rectors' conferences). The EUA's institutional evaluations (nearly 200 so far in European and some non-European countries) strike a fair balance between spontaneous commitment on the part of institutions (self-assessment reports) and outside experts' contributions. However, since institutions themselves commission these evaluations, nothing obliges them to act on the findings – which is certainly the main weakness of this approach. Things are different when, as has happened a couple of times in recent years, governments or government departments ask the EUA to assess institutions and their internal quality assurance procedures.

The fact that the standards and guidelines for quality assurance in the European Higher Education Area (2005), formulated by the European Association for Quality Assurance in Higher Education (ENQA) with its partners[2] as part of the Bologna process and at the request of the ministers of education, are infused with the same spirit augurs well for the development of a quality assurance strategy which both matches the nature of universities and is effective. Moreover, dynamic countries like Ireland organise quality assurance on these same principles, giving institutions extensive responsibility for regular assessment of their own faculties, departments, as well as services, and having their procedures assessed by an outside body, for example the EUA in 2005 (Irish Universities Quality Board (IUQB)[3]). Finally, we may note that a number of European universities have in recent years spontaneously devised internal faculty or department evaluation systems, based on self-assessment and inspection by experts.

We may also note the growing practice of assessing (some say accrediting) internal quality assessment procedures. However, the danger here is that quality measures may be seen as an end in themselves, having no connection with the institution's strategy and implementation of that strategy, that is, its response to the challenge of being able to change. The point should also be made that a few institutions find benchmarking useful. Assessment of teaching by students (practised systematically for a considerable time in some countries, not easily introduced in others) can also be very instructive, provided that questionnaires are well designed, and that those in charge of the subdivision – usually deans – take action on detected failings.

Our earlier discussion of the strategic choices involved in selecting an evaluation method suggests that accreditation systems may be open to some reservations. They may be broadly justified to protect consumers in the case of private institutions, but they must be flexibly applied – particularly to ensure that institutions which fail on one criterion, but score well on the others, are not refused accreditation. One interesting use

---

2. The European University Association (EUA), the European Association of Institutions in Higher Education (EURASHE) and the National Unions of Students in Europe (ESIB).
3. www.iuqb.ie.

of accreditation involves recognising institutions which attain a certain quality level, for example, the EQUIS (European Quality Improvement System), which applies to business schools. This gives institutions a further incentive to improve; nonetheless, it should not be substituted for formative assessment. The main reservation here concerns countries which subject all teaching programmes to accreditation. Under the subsidiarity principle – invoked by the ministers of education in Berlin (2003) – programme assessment should be the responsibility of the institutions themselves. More seriously, very few programmes are ever refused accreditation, which means that the system costs more than its results warrant. Accrediting whole institutions is still more questionable. This is probably justified for brand-new institutions, but certainly not for those which have been in place for decades, or indeed centuries – provided that outside agencies monitor their internal quality procedures and/or assess their capacity for change. This is an area where non-discriminatory and intelligent solutions must be found.

Let us hope that this chapter, which is the work of an academic involved in institutional evaluation procedures, will convince the sceptics that developing a culture of quality in view of improving it is essential, and also convince the perfectionists that institutions of higher education are complex, but generally mature entities. This being so, we must let them do the job they were meant to do – but not be afraid to subject them to regular professional scrutiny, so that they can remedy their failings and shortcomings?

References

Bergen communiqué (2005),
www.bologna-bergen2005.no/Docs/00-Main_doc/050520_Bergen_Communique.pdf

Berlin communiqué (2003), *Realising the European Higher Education Area*,
www.bologna-bergen2005.no/Docs/00-Main_doc/030919Berlin_Communique.PDF

Bologna declaration (1999),
www.bologna-bergen2005.no/Docs/00-Main_doc/990719BOLOGNA_
DECLARATION.PDF

ENQA, the European Association for Quality Assurance in Higher Education,
www.enqa.eu/

ENQA (2005), "Standards and Guidelines for Quality Assurance in the European Higher Education Area", www.enqa.eu/files/ENQA%20Bergen%20Report.pdf

EQUIS, the European Quality Improvement System of the European Foundation for Management Development, www.efmd.org/html/Accreditations/cont_detail.asp?id=0 40929rpku&aid=041029wupz&tid=1&ref=ind

ESIB, the National Unions of Students in Europe, www.esib.org/

EUA, the European University Association, www.eua.be/eua/index.jsp

EUA (2005), *Review of Quality Assurance in Irish Universities*, EUA Institutional Evaluation Programme, Brussels, www.iuqb.ie/

EURASHE, European Association of Institutions in Higher Education, www.eurashe.be/

IUQB, Irish Universities Quality Board, www.iuqb.ie/

Kohler, J. and Huber, J. (eds) (2006), *Higher education governance between democratic culture, academic aspiration and market forces*, Council of Europe Higher Education Series No. 5, Strasbourg

Perellon J.-F. (2003) *La qualité dans l'enseignement supérieur*, Le Savoir suisse.

Prague Communiqué (2001), www.bologna-bergen2005.no/Docs/00-Main_ doc/010519PRAGUE_COMMUNIQUE.PDF

Sorbonne Joint Declaration (1998), www.bologna-bergen2005.no/Docs/00-Main_ doc/980525SORBONNE_DECLARATION.PDF

UNESCO-Council of Europe (1997), *Convention on the Recognition of Qualifications concerning Higher Education in the European Region*, Paris/Strasbourg

UNESCO (1998), *World declaration on higher education for the twenty-first century: vision and action*, Paris

United Nations (1948), *Universal Declaration of Human Rights*, New York, www.un.org/Overview/rights.html

Vlasceanu, Lazar, Grunberg, Laura and Parlea, Dan (2004), *Quality Assurance and Accreditation: A Glossary of Basic Terms and Definitions*, UNESCO/CEPES, 2004

Weber, L. (2005), "Nature and scope of the public responsibility for higher education and research?" in Weber and Bergan (eds) *The public responsibility for higher education and research*, Council of Europe Higher Education Series No. 2, Strasbourg, pp. 29-43.

Weber, L. and Bergan, S. (eds) (2005), *The public responsibility for higher education and research,* Council of Europe Higher Education Series No. 2, Strasbourg

Weber, L. (2006a), "European university governance in urgent need of change", in Kohler and Huber (eds), *Higher education governance between democratic culture, academic aspiration and market forces*, Council of Europe Higher Education Series No. 5, Strasbourg, pp. 63-75

Weber, L. (2006b), "University governance, leadership and management in a rapidly changing environment" in L. Purser (ed.), *Understanding Bologna in Context*, European University Association and Raabe Academic Publishers, Brussels and Berlin, chapter A 2.2-1.

Role, responsibilities and means of public authorities and institutions: challenges in the light of a growing emphasis on market mechanisms

Alberto Amaral

> *Accountability and cynicism about human behaviour go hand in hand.*
> *(Martin Trow, 1996)*

1. Introduction

Quality mechanisms can have diverse objectives and uses in higher education, some more honourable than others. The different uses include improvement of institutions and study programmes, quality management, information to the public and "clients" in the emerging higher education markets, as a substitute for trust in institutions, to promote compliance with government objectives or government control, and even as a supranational policy enforcement tool (the Bologna Process and accreditation). However, the multiple uses and objectives of quality assessment can sometimes be contradictory.

The most frequently mentioned objectives of quality systems are quality improvement and accountability. Quality improvement addresses what Van Vught (1994) called the intrinsic dimension of higher education quality, which is mainly a concern of institutions, while the government pays special attention to accountability, which addresses the extrinsic dimensions of higher education quality, that is the qualities found in the services provided to society by higher education institutions.

Quality has always been a concern of universities. As Guy Neave recognised, "quality is not 'here to stay', if only for the self-evident reason that across the centuries of the university's existence in Europe, it never departed" (Neave 1994, p. 116).

In the Middle Ages it was already possible to distinguish three major models of quality assurance. The old universities of Oxford and Cambridge were self-governing communities of scholars that had the right to remove unsuitable masters and to co-opt new members using the equivalent of peer review mechanisms. The University of Paris, where the chancellor of the cathedral of Notre Dame had the power to decide about the content of studies, might be seen as the archetype of quality assessment in terms of accountability. And the model of the University of Bologna, ruled by students who hired the professors on an annual basis, controlling their assiduity and the quality of teaching, might be seen as an extreme example of the principles of customer satisfaction presently in vogue.

However, it was not until the early 1980s that quality became a public issue, giving rise to what Neave (1996) described as the emergence of the evaluative state. This can be explained by a number of convergent factors such as massification – which created much more heterogeneous higher education systems in terms of institutions, students and professors – the increasing role of market regulation, the emergence of new public management, and a loss of trust in higher education institutions and their professionals.

Being initially an almost exclusive concern of the academics, quality progressively became a matter of public concern in the 1980s and 1990s, the two main objectives of quality assessment being quality improvement and accountability. The balance between these conflicting objectives lies more on the side of improvement where academics had a strong voice, and more on the side of accountability when the will of the government predominated.

Quality systems, albeit in a number of different forms (quality assurance, accreditation, licensing, etc.), are today an intrusive reality of every national higher education system and will remain an important regulation and steering tool for many governments. And it is possible to detect that trust in institutions has not been restored, as there is an apparent movement from quality assessment as a tool for improvement to accreditation as a tool for customer protection and accountability.

2. The emergence of markets in higher education

Competition is not new in universities. Students have long competed with each other for access to scarce university places and professors are used to competition for academic distinction on the basis of their published research and scholarship (Dill et al., 2004, p. 327). What is new is the use of market mechanisms as a tool for increasing the efficiency of public services – including higher education – to maximise the provision of social benefits.

In many countries governments have been experimenting with market-type mechanisms to force higher education institutions to compete for students, for funds, for research money. Even the Bologna Declaration "redefining the nature and content of academic programmes is transforming what were once state monopolies over academic degrees into competitive international markets" (Dill et al., 2004, p. 330).

The emergence of the market in higher education gives legitimacy to state intervention to avoid the negative effects of market competition and to create conditions for their efficient operation, which includes the need for consumer information. Disclosing the results of quality assessment of institutions and programmes and providing an array of performance indicators are information tools frequently used by the state.

The supposed social benefits of markets cannot in fact be realised without appropriate government regulations setting the rules for the effective operation of markets, minimising the production of socially unacceptable distribution outcomes in terms of equity and avoiding the emergence of monopolies. For Boyer and Drache, in the absence of surveillance mechanisms, market competition might "severely distort the alleged smooth adjustment process of supply and demand" (2000, pp. 6-7).

For the allocation of goods and services to be "optimally efficient for the larger society" (Leslie and Johnson, 1974) the market needs to be perfectly competitive, which implies a number of conditions that are difficult to fulfil. Indeed, both government and market regulation may lead to inefficient action, as is well documented in the literature.

Non-market or government failures are related to the fact that sometimes the government and its agencies are incapable of perfect performance in designing and implementing public policy, because of defects of representative democracy and inefficiencies of public agencies to produce and to distribute goods and services (Dill, 1997; Van Vught, 1997).

Market failures are the shortcomings of markets (Van Vught, 1997) when confronted with certain goods and conditions, namely the production of goods that show large externalities,[4] as is the case of education. As the market is a means of organising the exchange of goods and services based upon price, additional social benefits (externalities) will tend to be ignored, or to be insufficiently taken into account by market mechanisms. Other sources of market failures are the tendency of a free market to build monopolies resulting in inefficient outcomes – in general, government regulation outlaws this kind of development in order to protect consumers – or the so-called "market imperfections" (Van Vught, 1997) such as prices not reflecting product scarcities and insufficient or asymmetric information.

For efficient market operation there is a need for perfect information by producers and consumers about price, quality and other relevant characteristics of the good or service being purchased for a market to produce efficient outcomes. However, in many cases, the relevant information is not available (imperfect information) or the producer has a much more detailed knowledge than the consumer (asymmetric information).

The information problem is particularly acute in the case of higher education, which has three simultaneous characteristics. First, it is an experience good, meaning that its relevant characteristics can only be effectively assessed by consumption, as it is only after a student starts attending a study programme that he/she gets a real idea of what has been purchased in terms of quality, professors, and the general value of its educational experience. Second, it is a rare purchase, as in most cases a student enrols in a single study programme throughout his/her professional life and cannot derive market experience from frequent purchases. Finally, opting-out costs are high, as it is generally rather expensive to change to a different study programme or institution (Dill and Soo, 2004).

---

4. The concept of externality is used to compare the social and private benefits of any activity, and can be technically defined as the benefit received by society beyond the individual private benefit.

The simultaneous presence of these three characteristics makes a strong case for government intervention to protect consumers, which may take different forms such as licensing, accreditation, and the public disclosure of the results of quality assessment activities, all of them aimed at increasing consumer information (Smith, 2000), which justifies the increasing role of quality assessment for market regulation purposes.

However, Dill still considered that from the strict point of view of "rational economic choice", "students lack sufficient information about the quality of academic institutions or programs to make discriminating choices" (1997, p. 180) as what they needed was the measure of prospective future earnings provided by alternative academic programmes and not "peer review evaluation of teaching processes, nor subjective judgements of the quality of a curriculum" (ibid.).

On the other hand, even if these kind of data were available, many students (or their families) would not use them, which questions the validity of the hypothesis of rational economic choice (Tavares et al., 2006). Although students were free to choose any study programme, choices were made, as Bourdieu (1989) argued, using criteria learned and inherited at social level. Students linked choice with accessibility (Gottfredson, 1981, p. 548), which related to obstacles or opportunities in a social or economic context that affected possibilities of integrating a particular job. That is why Bourdieu (1982) advocated that the educational system reproduced the social structure.

This is what David Dill called the problem of immature consumers and provides the ground for "the implementation of quasi-markets, rather than consumer-oriented markets, for the distribution of academic programs" (Dill, 1997, p. 181). The state or a state agency, acting on behalf of the final consumers, can get a better bargain from the providers as it has a much stronger power of the purse than any individual client, a logic that is reinforced when (immature) clients do not make rational choices. The state is no longer a provider of higher education but assumes a role as principal, representing the interests of the consumers by making contracts with competing institutions, which creates a quasi-market in which independent providers compete with each other in an internal market (Le Grand and Bartlett, 1993).

3. Institutional autonomy and markets

The implementation of markets needs providers and consumers to have a number of freedoms (Jongbloed 2003); for instance, providers need to be free to enter the market, to determine prices and to specify the products, while consumers should be free to choose the product and the provider and to have adequate information on prices and quality. Therefore the implementation of markets in higher education has been accompanied by increasing institutional autonomy, which allowed institutions to compete by deciding what programmes to offer, their characteristics, and eventually the level of fees, although in practice – with the usual exception of the US – the state still heavily regulates some of these institutional freedoms.

Public universities receive at least a significant part of their budgets from the state under the argument that they further the public good by contributing to economic development and by advancing the life prospects of citizens by increasing their "employability" potential, to use the new European terminology. Public universities are non-profit organisations that are by law forced to reinvest any surplus in the organisation itself instead of ending up in private benefits for its members. This in principle offers the state some guarantee that the organisation will not digress from its obligation of upholding the public good. And it explains why the state, at least in most European countries, mistrusts private higher education institutions and either forbids them or tries to control them more closely than it does for public institutions (Teixeira and Amaral, 2001).

However, the increased institutional autonomy combined with market competition may lead to serious difficulties in market regulation, as autonomous institutions forced to compete in a market may follow strategies aiming at ensuring their own development and survival, which may lead to strategies contrary to the public good or the government's objectives.

Massy (2004b, p. 28) argued that "the way institutions currently respond to markets and seek internal efficiencies, left unchecked, is unlikely to serve the public good", a danger that is exacerbated when competition is excessive, or when the state cuts public subsidies thus curtailing the institutional capacity for discretionary spending. By using the microeconomic theory of non-profit enterprises, Massy (2004a) demonstrated that under those conditions institutions tend to behave like for-profit ones, ignoring the promotion of the public good inherent to their missions. This forces the state to intervene by changing the rules of the market to ensure the fulfilment of its own political objectives, quality assessment being one of the tools that might be used to ensure the compliance of institutions with public policies.

4. Quasi-markets and the principal–agent dilemma

When quasi-markets are implemented, the government agencies making the purchases in the name of consumers face the classic principal–agent dilemma: "how the principal [government] can best motivate the agent [university] to perform as the principal would prefer, taking into account the difficulties in monitoring the agent's activities" (Sappington, 1991, p. 45, cited in Dill and Soo, 2004, p. 58).

The principal–agent problem is exacerbated when providers have considerable autonomy and may result in contradictions of neo-liberal policies. On the one hand, neo-liberalism claims that government intervention is the mother of all sins and that institutions should be allowed to operate freely under the rules of market competition. On the other hand, the government realises that autonomous institutions competing in a market may behave in ways that are contrary to public policies and the public good. This leads to the arbitrary intrusion of the government to change the rules of the game in order to force the institutions to follow strategies that in some cases are even self-defeating from a pure market perspective.

Ben Jongbloed (2004, pp. 89-90) used a traffic metaphor to clarify the differences between the traditional government model of centralised command and control (similar to traffic signals) to co-ordinate higher education systems and the adoption of market-based policies (similar to a roundabout). In Jongbloed's metaphor, traffic lights condition drivers' decisions heavily, in the same way that government regulation conditions the behaviour of institutions. On the other hand, a roundabout, while influencing traffic behaviour, delegates decision-making authority to the drivers (Dill et al., 2004, p. 329). However, Dominique Orr (2004), taking into account the difficulties of state steering of autonomous institutions in a market, suggests that the new relationship between the higher education institutions and the government is better portrayed by the "roundabout model" (Jongbloed, 2003) but with an increasing number of [government] traffic lights restricting the allowed routes.

This is consistent with the idea that effective delegation of "public-interest decision-making" authority to institutions requires "an affirmative desire to interpret and serve the public good, the will to hold institutional self-interest at bay, and the financial strength to balance intrinsic values with market forces" (Massy 2004b, p. 33). However, the unchecked behaviour of institutions, especially under conditions of strong competition and financial stringency, may not correspond to the best public interest, which paves the way for further government intervention.

That is why governments have been introducing an increasing number of mechanisms to ensure that institutions will behave in the way the government wants them to do. Among these mechanisms there is an extensive array of performance indicators and measures of academic quality, be it called quality assurance or accreditation. Therefore, quality assessment can be used as a compliance tool.

5. The loss of trust

Any specific discussion of higher education management needs to be set within the broader context of new public management and related concepts, such as new managerialism and reinventing government (Osborne and Gaebler, 1992), which have dominated public sector reform over the last two decades. As Denhardt and Denhardt (2000, p. 1) noted, "the New Public Management has championed a vision of public managers as the entrepreneurs of a new, leaner, and increasingly privatised government, emulating not only the practices but also the values of business".

Under new public management the public are clients of the government, and administrators should seek to deliver services that satisfy clients. In higher education, too, students are referred to as customers or clients, and in most higher education systems quality assurance and accountability measures have been put in place to ensure that academic provision meets client needs and expectations.

One of the consequences of new public management policies appears to be a strong attack on professions, including the academic profession. Reed (2002, p. 166) stated:

> By imposing market competition through political dictate and administrative fiat, the ideology of 'new managerialism' attempted to destroy, or at least weaken, the regulatory structures that had protected unaccountable professional elites and their monopolistic labour market and work practices across the full range of public sector service provision throughout the 1980s and 1990s.

Traditional university governance also has become the target of fierce criticism, and the multi-secular tradition of collegial governance is today considered inefficient and corporative, and many governments yielded to the temptation of improving university management. Models were imported from the corporate world trying to replace the slow, inefficient decision-making processes of academic collegiality by the "fast, adventurous, carefree, gung-ho, open-plan, computerised individualism of choice, autonomous enterprises and sudden opportunity" (Ball, 1998, p. 124). The reinforced presence of external stakeholders in university governance intended to promote responsiveness to the "external world" (Magalhães and Amaral, 2000) and appointed presidents with sound managerial curricula are replacing elected academics at the rudder of the university vessel.

Entrepreneurial values and attitudes are being forced upon the academics, and tenure is being abolished on the grounds that it inhibits the business spirit (Torres and Schugurensky, 2002). The development of academic capitalism (Slaughter and Leslie, 1999) and the introduction of market-like competition mechanisms forced professors, departments, and faculties increasingly to engage "in competitive behaviour similar to the one prevailing in the marketplace for funding, grants, contracts, and student selection and funding" (Torres and Schugurensky, 2002, p. 446).

The academy no longer enjoys great prestige on which higher education can build a successful claim to political autonomy (Scott 1989). Academics are no longer seen as disinterested professionals fully dedicated to the production of new knowledge but rather as being suppliers of services to clients – the students – and as such no longer deserving the unrestricted trust of society. Academic capitalism (Slaughter and Leslie, 1999) also made faculty more like all other workers, making faculty, staff and students less like university professionals and more like corporate professionals whose discoveries are considered work-for-hire, the property of the corporation, not the professional. This change from professional to mere employee status has forced academics to be "expected to respond to penalties and incentives devised by the funding agency, required like any other employee of the state to account for themselves and their behavior to a bureaucracy" (Trow 1996).

The "de-professionalisation" of academics has been coupled with a claim to professional status by administrative staff. Thirty years ago administrators were "very much expected to operate in a subservient supportive role to the academic community, very much in a traditional Civil Servant mould" (Amaral et al., 2003, p. 286) and in the meetings of academia they were expected to be seen but not to be heard. Today, managers see themselves as essential contributors to the successful functioning of the contemporary university.

The emergence of the new public management and the attacks on the efficiency of public services, including higher education, resulted in loss of trust in institutions and professionals, and in the gradual proletarisation of the academic professions – an erosion of their relative class and status advantages (Halsey, 1992). For Trow (1996) every institution is linked to its surroundings through some combination of accountability, market and trust. Accountability is the obligation to report to others, to explain, to justify, answering questions about how resources have been used, and to what effect (Trow, 1996); the link of higher education to society through the market is visible when support is provided to a college or university in return for the immediate provision of goods or services; trust is visible in the provision of support, by either public or private bodies, without the requirement that the institutions either provide specific goods and services in return for that support, or account specifically and in detail for the use of those funds. The laws of autonomy or envelope budgeting are examples of trust. For Trow (1996) accountability is an alternative to trust, and efforts to strengthen it usually involve parallel efforts to weaken trust, and he adds that accountability and cynicism about human behaviour go hand in hand.

It is true that the loss of trust was not only the result of public policies derived from new public management. The massification of higher education systems was accompanied by a large increase in the heterogeneity of both students and professors, and by the emergence of new institutional forms much different from the elite university. All this has led to a decline of trust in higher education systems, their institutions and their professionals and has paved the way to quality assessment mechanisms (Trow, 1996).

6. The Bologna Process and a stratified European Higher Education Area

The Bologna Process, which aims at building the European Higher Education Area (EHEA), was an initiative of European states to converge their higher education structures. In March 2000, the European Council presented the Lisbon strategy to make the EU the world's most dynamic and competitive economy. Under this strategy, a stronger economy will drive job creation alongside social and environmental policies to ensure sustainable development and social inclusion (Veiga and Amaral, 2006).

Empirical evidence points to the possibility that the Bologna Process and the Lisbon strategy, although different in nature and in objectives, are now converging into one policy framework (van der Wende and Huisman, 2004, p. 2) that may increase the relevance of the economic factors in European policies, while inducing a move of higher education from a paradigm of co-operation to a paradigm of competition. The decision of the Commission to finance a prospective study of a qualification system of higher education institutions, the document "Best use of resources", the participation of international agencies in rankings of higher education institutions and the way the European accreditation system might develop are all indications of a stratified European Higher Education Area.

The new European Higher Education Area that the Bologna process aims to implement will be a complex system of very diverse institutions, offering a wide range of quality. It can be observed that there is a more neo-liberal model that occasionally becomes visible in European policies. This model tends to emphasise the importance of the efficiency of the system, as can be seen from a document of the European Commission (2004a) entitled "Making the best use of resources" stating:

> "The necessary level and type of investment and their consequent impact on efficiency depend on the development level of the country as defined by its proximity to the technology frontier (i.e. relative to the technologically most advanced countries). Countries far from the frontier should focus on primary and secondary education (imitation process), whereas countries close to the frontier should invest primarily in higher education (innovation process)."

There are other developments, such as the recent paper "Institutional profiles, towards a typology of higher education institutions in Europe", supported by the Commission, which proposed a European higher education typology – even if its authors stated that it should be emphasised right away that the European higher education typology was not an instrument for ranking higher education institutions, and the recent and growing interest of organisations such as UNESCO and the OCDE in the rankings of higher education institutions.

The massification of the European higher education systems has created new problems. Trow (1996, p. 320) recognised:

> "The growth and diversification of higher education, along with associated changes in pedagogy, will require that a society and its systems of higher education surrender any idea of broad common standards of academic performance between institutions, and even between subjects within a single university – ministerial assertions to the contrary notwithstanding."

This is a criticism of the stubborn attitude of many European governments in considering that all their national higher education institutions offer similar quality, an attitude that clearly contrasts with that of the Americans who "never made (or could make) any commitment as a nation to the maintenance of common standards across our thousands of colleges and universities" (Trow, 1996, p. 319).

These developments can be linked to the efforts of the European Commission in the area of accreditation, although they were met with opposition from many higher education institutions and mistrust from governments. As recently as 2001, at the end of the Bologna meeting of education ministers held in Prague, it was recognised in the final report that no consensus on accreditation had been possible:

"The question of who is responsible for setting the reference standards has proved to be a delicate and controversial one, especially if it is considered at European level. Alongside those that firmly believe in accreditation, even at European level, there are those that fear externally imposed European standards as inadequate to their national system or reality and a restriction to the institutional capacity to innovate" (Lourtie, 2001, p. 16).

However, despite the opposition of a large number of higher education institutions and the distrust of some ministers the idea of European accreditation has survived all difficulties, and in 2004 the European Commission (2004b) presented a proposal for a recommendation of the Council and of the European Parliament. According to the proposal, there will be multiple accreditation agencies, public and private, national and international that need to be recognised by a central agency. Higher education institutions should be allowed by their governments to choose any agency they prefer. This is consistent with the idea of a stratified European Area of Higher Education, as institutions would be allowed to choose an accreditation agency adequate to their quality level. It is possible to foresee that some accreditation agencies will address excellence at an international level while others will be more appropriate to regional or local institutions, some will accredit research universities while others will specialise in teaching-only institutions.

Therefore, it is possible to conclude that quality assessment can also be used as a tool for the implementation of supranational policies. In the case of the Bologna Process, probably under the influence of the more economic emphasis of the Lisbon strategy, "efficiency" is increasingly becoming a new buzzword, while some instruments leading to the emergence of a European market for higher education are taking form, which corresponds to a move from a co-operation paradigm to a competition paradigm.

7. Some concluding remarks

The first concluding remark is that there is an indisputable responsibility and legitimacy of public authorities in guaranteeing the quality of higher education. This will be the case when the model of relationship between institutions and government is one of centralised state control, but also the case when institutions are autonomous and the market plays a role. In the latter case the state needs to regulate the market to avoid socially unacceptable distribution outcomes in terms of equity. The recent Portuguese experience showed that market mechanisms are complex, constitute a learning process that cannot be expected to produce effective regulation instantly, and they should not be played by wizard's apprentices. Moreover, as is the case of Portugal, where those mechanisms only play a secondary role in the regulation of the system, there is a regulatory role of the state that the government should not forsake. An effective and active regulation by the state, clarifying and endorsing the rules of the system, can take advantage of the benefits of those market-like mechanisms. Otherwise it will drive the higher education system onto a complicated course.

However, much will depend on the uses and objectives of the quality assurance system to be implemented, as well as on its mechanisms and ownership. For the time being it is apparent that in Europe there is a movement towards systems based on accreditation mechanisms.

The Council of Europe has produced two timely and important documents, one on Public Responsibility for Higher Education and Research, the other on Higher Education Governance. It is important to stress two fundamental ideas: that governance should avoid micromanagement, leaving reasonable scope for innovation and flexibility, and that quality assessment mechanisms should be built on trust and give due regard to internal quality development processes. No doubt every academic will strongly support these ideas based on elevated and generous principles.

The second concluding remark refers to the use of micromanagement mechanisms as a governance tool in higher education. Unfortunately, higher education institutions are increasingly using micromanagement mechanisms in order to respond to outside (state) pressures, which promote the new values and demands of "economy, efficiency, utility, public accountability, enterprise and various definitions of quality". Management control technologies include systems for evaluation and performance measurement of research, teaching and some administrative activities, particularly those linked to finance. The implementation of these systems occurs in basic units, which are internally made accountable for budget expenditure (eventually decentralised) and for the results of evaluations of teaching and research activities. The influence of the recommendations (or sanctions) from those evaluations is one of the most important aspects determining the selection and concentration of activities (Meek, 2002) in higher education institutions, as well as on the degree of autonomy of professionals. For instance, in the United Kingdom control mechanisms included an extremely detailed framework of devolved performance criteria against which operational efficiency and effectiveness at the unit level would be monitored and assessed (Reed, 2002).

In the case of Europe, the Lisbon strategy has created a problem of policy implementation as it has invaded areas that in principle fall under the exclusive competence of national states. In 2000 the Lisbon European Council formally adopted the Open Method of Co-ordination (OMC) to enlarge intervention to other policy areas: information society, research, innovation, enterprise policy, education and social exclusion (Veiga and Amaral, 2006).

OMC is a new soft law procedure assuming policy implementation as a logical and rational top-down linear process from the Commission to states, institutions and citizens. It differs from the traditional Community method (Schäfer, 2004, p. 1) as it tries to implement "policy reforms without confronting the deep normative, perhaps even ideological, fracture over the model of capitalism most suitable for the EU" (Radaelli, 2003, p. 20).

The introduction of a soft law procedure (OMC) in social policy contrasts with the hard law in monetary and fiscal policies. Schäfer (2004) argued this is the result of the emerging confrontation between a neo-liberal model and a more social model in European policies, emphasised by the Lisbon strategy, which did not allow for a new Maastricht-type consensus.

Gornitzka (2005, p. 7) has further elaborated on the OMC lack of formal constraints, of legal sanctions and of formal policy co-ordination, and states:

> "The normative pressure stemming from a desire to look good or fear of being embarrassed may be a strong mechanism for converging with the European definition of good policies and striving for performing well on the indicators in cases where it is considered important to keep up with the 'European Joneses'"

although Kok (2004, p. 43) recognised:

> "More than a hundred indicators have been associated with the Lisbon process, which makes it likely that every country will be ranked as best at one indicator or another. This makes this instrument ineffective."

Therefore, it can be seen that the use of performance indicators and benchmarks are becoming a common practice in European policy implementation, which is congruent with the implementation of accreditation mechanisms, rankings of institutions and the emergence of a stratified EHEA.

The last concluding remark goes to accreditation and trust. There is today a tendency for a change from quality assessment mechanisms to accreditation, at the European level as well as at the level of its member states. The US is the country with the most well-established tradition of accreditation, which makes it interesting to analyse the developments in that country. David Dill (1996), writing about institutional self-regulation in the US, casts doubts about the adequacy of the current processes and standards of US academic accreditation and refers to the failure of voluntary accreditation in solving the inadequacy of collegial mechanisms of educational quality assurance. This was also the opinion of Martin Trow (1994), who considered:

> "to a considerable extent, external academic accountability in the US, mainly in the form of accreditation, has been irrelevant to the improvement of higher education; in some cases it has acted more to shield institutions from effective monitoring of their own educational performance than to provide it; in still other cases it distinctly hampers the efforts of institutions to improve themselves. It encourages institutions to report their strengths rather than their weaknesses, their successes rather than their failures – and even to conceal their weaknesses and failures from view".

Elaine El-Khawas (1993) also described some areas of weakness of the US accreditation system, such as the "accommodationalist" approach of judging an institution entirely in terms of its chosen mission, and the poor quality of evidence presented by the institutions for accrediting. This resulted from the need to acknowledge differences in institutional type and mission within a very diversified system. In practice, all accredited institutions in a given region carried the same imprimatur, although in practice different standards were applied to different types of institutions (only the Western Association of Schools and Colleges had one commission to review colleges and universities and another to review community and junior colleges).

This raises a fundamental question of trust. Quality improvement needs a critical self-evaluation report, which will be difficult to obtain when the system contains an element of punishment such as resource allocation based on the results of evaluation, and Trow (1994) argued that the problem would be "to create a system of accountability that does not punish truth telling and reward the appearance of achievement". To solve this problem Dill et al. recommended that the route to quality assurance must combine "a mutually reinforcing system of institution-based quality assessments of teaching and learning and a system of external academic audits". A similar proposal was made by Trow (1994), who suggested that the role of outside supranational, governmental or quasi-governmental agencies should consist of "monitoring and encouraging the emergence of this culture in institutions of mass higher education, but not through 'evaluations' based on uniform criteria and linked to funding" (Trow, ibid.). This is much more consistent with "quality audit" than with quality assessment or accreditation (Amaral, 2001).

This means that several authors recommended that in the US the responsibility for creating the necessary mechanisms for quality assessment and quality improvement should lie with each and every institution, and that outside independent agencies, such as the already existing six regional accrediting associations, should assume the role of meta-evaluating or auditing.

However, apparently the EU has opted for accreditation, which probably translates as an increasing mistrust of institutions and academic peer review methods, a trend that is being followed by a number of European countries. Even in countries where institutions had been able to beat the government at its own game to gain ownership over the quality assessment system – a good example is provided by the Dutch case – there is now a movement towards accreditation. By claiming that the major responsibility for quality lay with the institutions themselves, and that trust in the supportive character of the quality assessment exercise was a necessary condition for open and critical self-assessment – a fundamental tool for improvement – Dutch universities were able to convince the ministry that they should control the quality assurance system through an "independent" agency, the VSNU. The Portuguese universities have followed the same road, and the Evaluation of Higher Education Act (Law 38/94 of 21 November) has given the ownership of the quality agency to "representative institutions", which in the case of public universities was the "Foundation of Portuguese Universities", similar to the Dutch VSNU. However, there is today a Dutch accreditation system, while the Portuguese Government has asked ENQA for technical support for creating an accreditation agency meeting the standards and guidelines for quality assurance in the European Higher Education Area.

Options for the future of a quality system are not separated from considerations of the type of higher education system the relevant authorities want to foster. Apparently the objective of Brussels puts more emphasis on competition and the creation of a European Higher Education Area than on co-operation and quality improvement.

The growing emphasis on market mechanisms, new public management and competition accompanied by the loss of trust in institutions and the proletarisation of academics may well lead to developments in an opposite direction to that proposed in the documents produced by the Council of Europe.

Therefore I would like to end with an appeal to the Council of Europe to remain attentive to developments taking place in European higher education and to use its moral and legitimate power to ensure that the European Higher Education Area will become an example to the world by preserving the core values of universities in this new world where the human being is seen as a trader, persistently engaged in making judgements about the economic advantages and disadvantages of various courses of action (Drache, 2001).

References

Amaral, A., Fulton, O. and Larsen, I.M. (2003), "A managerial revolution?" In Amaral, A., Meek, V.L. and Larsen, I.M. (eds), *The Higher Education Managerial Revolution?*, Kluwer Academic Publishers, Dordrecht, pp. 275-96.

Amaral, A. (2001), "Higher education in the process of European integration, globalizing economies and mobility of students and staff", in Huisman, J. and Maassen, P. (eds), *Higher Education and the Nation State*, Pergamon, London.

Amaral, A. and Teixeira, P. (2000), "The rise and fall of the private sector in Portuguese higher education?", *Higher Education Policy*, 13.3, pp. 245-66.

Amaral, A. (1998), "The US accreditation system and the CRE's quality audits – a comparative study", *Quality Assurance in Education*, 6.4.

Ball, S.J. (1998), "Big policies/small world: an introduction to international perspectives in education policy", *Comparative Education*, 34.2, pp. 119-30.

Bourdieu, P. and Passeron, J.C. (1982), *A Reprodução*, Francisco Alves, Rio de Janeiro.

Bourdieu, P. (1989), *La Noblesse d'État – Grandes écoles et esprit de corps*, Les Éditions de Minuit, Paris.

Boyer, R. and Drache, D. (eds) (2000), *States Against Markets*, Routledge, New York, 4th edition.

Denhardt, R.B. and Denhardt, J. (2000), "The new public service: serving rather than steering", *Public Administration Review*, 60.6, pp. 1-24.

Dill, D., Massy, W.F., Williams, P.-R. and Cook, C.M. (1996), "Accreditation & academic quality assurance – can we get there from here?", *Change*, September/October, pp. 17-24.

Dill, D. (1997), "Higher education markets and public policy", *Higher Education Policy*, 10.3/4, pp. 167-85.

Dill, D. and Soo, M. (2004), "Transparency and quality in higher education markets", in Teixeira, P., Jongbloed, B., Dill, D. and Amaral, A. (eds), *Markets in Higher Education: Rhetoric or Reality?*, Kluwer Academic Publishers, Dordrecht, pp. 61-85.

Dill, D., Teixeira, P., Jongbloed, B. and Amaral, A. (2004), "Conclusions", in Teixeira, P., Jongbloed, B., Dill, D. and Amaral, A. (eds), *Markets in Higher Education: Rhetoric or Reality?*, Kluwer Academic Publishers, Dordrecht, pp. 327-52.

El-Khawas, E. (1993), "Accreditation and evaluation: reciprocity and exchange", in *Conference on Frameworks for European Quality Assessment of Higher Education*, Copenhagen.

European Commission, Directorate General Education and Culture (2004a), *Implementation of "Education & Training 2010" Work Programme, Working Group E – "Making the Best Use of Resources"*, Progress Report, December.

European Commission (2004b), *Proposal for a Recommendation of the Council and the European Parliament on further co-operation in quality assurance in higher education*, Brussels, 12.10.2004, COM(2004) 642 final.

Gottfredson, L. (1981), "Circumscription and compromise: a developmental theory of occupational aspirations", *Journal of Counseling Psychology,* 28.6, pp. 545-79.

Halsey, A.H. (1992), *Decline of Donnish Dominion: The British Academic Professions in the Twentieth Century*, Clarendon Press, Oxford.

Jongbloed, B. (2003), "Marketisation in higher education: Clark's triangle and the essential ingredients of markets", *Higher Education Quarterly*, 57.2, pp. 110-35.

Jongbloed, B. (2004), "Regulation and competition in higher education", in Teixeira, P., Jongbloed, B., Dill, D. and Amaral, A. (eds), *Markets in Higher Education: Rhetoric or Reality?*, Kluwer Academic Publishers, Dordrecht, pp. 87-111.

Kok, W. (2004), *Facing the challenge – the Lisbon strategy for growth and employment*, Luxembourg, European Communities.

Le Grand, J. and Bartlett, W. (1993), *Quasi-Markets and Social Policy*, Macmillan Press, London.

Lourtie, P. (rapporteur), Report to the ministers of education of the signatory countries, Prague, May 2001.

Magalhães, A. and Amaral, A. (2000), "Portuguese higher education and the imaginary friend: the stakeholder's role in institutional governance", *European Journal of Education*, 35.4, pp. 439-48.

Massy, W.F. (2004a), "Markets in higher education: do they promote internal efficiency?", in Teixeira, P., Jongbloed, B., Dill, D. and Amaral, A. (eds), *Markets in Higher Education: Rhetoric or Reality?*, Kluwer Academic Publishers, Dordrecht, pp. 13-35.

Massy, W.F. (2004b), "Collegium Economicum: why institutions do what they do?", *Change*, 36.4, pp. 26-35.

Neave, G. (1994), "The politics of quality: developments in higher education in Western Europe 1992-1994", *European Journal of Education*, 29(2), pp. 115-33.

Orr, D. (2004), "More competition in German higher education: expectations, developments, outcomes", paper presented at the 17th CHER Conference, Enschede, 17-19 September.

Osborne, D. and Gaebler, T. (2002), *Re-inventing Government: How the Entrepreneurial Spirit is Transforming the Government*, Addison-Wesley, Reading, MA.

Radaelli, C. (2003), "The open method of co-ordination: a new governance architecture of analysis", SIEPS, Oslo.

Reed, M. (2002), "New managerialism, professional power and organisational governance in UK universities: a review and assessment", in Amaral, A., Jones, G.A. and Karseth, B. (eds), *Governing Higher Education: National Perspectives on Institutional Governance*, Kluwer Academic Publishers, Dordrecht, pp. 163-86.

Schäfer, A. (2004), "Beyond the community method: why the open method of co-ordination was introduced to EU policy-making", EIOP.

Scott, P. (1989), "The power of ideas", in Ball, C. and Eggins, H. (eds), *Higher Education into the 1990s: New Dimensions*, Society for Research into Higher Education and Open University Press, Buckingham, pp. 7-16.

Slaughter, S. and Leslie, L. (1999), *Academic Capitalism: Politics, Policies and the Entrepreneurial University*, Johns Hopkins Press, Baltimore.

Tavares, D., Lopes, O., Justino, E. and Amaral, A. (2006), "Students' preferences and needs in Portuguese higher education", paper presented at the 2006 EAIR annual conference, Rome.

Teixeira, P. and Amaral, A. (2001), "Private higher education and diversity: an exploratory survey", *Higher Education Quarterly*, 55.4, pp. 359-95.

Torres, C.A. and Schugurensky, D. (2002), "The political economy of higher education in the era of neoliberal globalization: Latin America in comparative perspective", *Higher Education,* 43, pp. 429-55.

Trow, M. (1994), "Managerialism and the academic profession: the case of England", *Higher Education Policy*, 7.2, pp. 11-18.

Trow, M. (1996), "Trust, markets and accountability in higher education: a comparative perspective", *Higher Education Policy*, 9.4, pp. 309-24.

van der Wende, M. and Huisman, J. (2004), "Europe", in Huisman, J. and van der Wende, M. (eds), *On cooperation and competition: National and European policies for the internationalisation of higher education*, Lemmens Verlag, Bonn.

Van Vught, F. (1997), "Combining planning and the market: an analysis of the government strategy towards higher education in the Netherlands", *Higher Education Policy*, 10.3/4, pp. 211-24.

Veiga, A. and Amaral, A. (2006), "The open method of coordination and the implementation of the Bologna Process", *Tertiary Education Management* (forthcoming).

The role of national quality assurance agencies in developing coherent, successful and competitive learning organisations in the European Higher Education Area

Ossi V. Lindqvist

One of the key elements in setting up the European Higher Education Area (EHEA) is the quality of higher education and the development of quality assurance (QA) systems for the higher education institutions. In Bergen in 2005, the European ministers adopted the standards and guidelines for quality assurance in the European Higher Education Area, as proposed by ENQA. The assessment of the progress on quality assurance will again be on the agenda in London in 2007. Earlier, in Berlin in 2003, the ministers had agreed that the national QA systems should include a "system of accreditation, certification or comparable procedures".

The development of QA systems in European countries, that is, the Bologna signatory countries, is well under way, though a lot is still to be achieved. Considerable variation exists in the higher education systems, with some countries having numerous private institutions, established especially after 1990, whereas in some countries all the institutions are publicly funded and thus legitimised by their respective higher education laws. The new private higher education institutions may need (public) accreditation for the sake of recognition of their degrees, or being included in the European mobility system, or for receiving public/governmental support.

There is wide agreement that the ENQA standards and guidelines for quality assurance in the European Higher Education Area[5] provide the basic framework for a possible overall QA system for the Bologna countries. However, it also leaves room for diversified national circumstances in terms of the very nature and details of the processes and, even in terms of the interpretation of "common" terminology; the same terms may have very different connotations in different countries and in different cultural contexts.

It is noteworthy that QA is clearly becoming a prime issue in the implementation of the EHEA, especially if one reads the tone of the ministers' Bergen communiqué (2005) correctly. Success in the implementation of the QA systems carries implications into student and staff mobility, degree structure and the recognition of degrees and study periods, all of which will be the key characteristics of the EHEA. And finally, one consequence should be an overall enhanced attractiveness of the EHEA. Stocktaking of these developments is due to take place in the ministerial conference in London in May 2007.

Yet the developments of the QA systems in Europe face problems and challenges which have to be solved or at least analytically recognised. These tasks may be related

---

5. www.enqa.eu/pubs.lasso.

to the QA concept itself, which takes different interpretations in different countries and contexts; or to the variability of the European higher education institutions as such which relates to their historical backgrounds, their financial structures, degree of autonomy, and so on. Finally, global developments in the form of heightened competition in the higher education market provide new challenges which QA developments must take into serious consideration.

One natural trend that was actually the impetus for quality assurance was the massification of higher education, which started in Europe in the 1970s and intensified in the 1980s and thereafter. Western Europe had a kind of boom in the establishment of new universities and polytechnics, especially in the 1960s and thereafter, to meet the new demand for higher education. Partly it was the result of the post-war baby boom and subsequent large classes. This increase in student volumes brought into higher education a new kind of student, who often did not have an academic background in the family, and in this sense the education he/she received carried a relatively high added value. But it also put new pressures on the teaching function in universities. Similarly, the teachers and professors themselves were increasingly hired from this new group of graduates and young scientists. This situation thus created and supported a new kind of social mobility in society, though its effects apparently were not equally strong in every European country. Higher education was thus seen more as a right for everybody rather than as a privilege for the few. In the US the same massification had started even earlier, right after the Second World War, and it was supported by the GI Bill of Rights of 1944, which gave educational benefits to the homecoming veterans and a chance for them to enter colleges and universities.

In eastern Europe this development was partly delayed, since virtually no new universities were established until approximately 1990. The situation almost "exploded" in those countries after the end of the Soviet era. Numerous private teaching institutions were born, and new programmes, especially in social sciences and business management, were added either simply because they were in high demand and/or there were paying "customers". With time, "natural" selection has eliminated many of these private institutions or they have been incorporated as semi-private units into the public higher education systems, often through various kinds of accreditation process. Especially for eastern European higher education institutions, periodic accreditation remains the major form of quality assurance and quality management.

The same massification of higher education started in the late 1990s in Asia, and especially in China and India. This development has been further intensified in the current decade. Comments have even been made of a partial "reverse" of the brain drain, whereby many Chinese and Indian people trained abroad are returning to their home countries to acquire expert positions in their universities, research institutes, or businesses.

Thus the global situation in higher education can be described as one of an increasing imbalance between demand and supply of higher education. This is also creating a truly international market for higher education, and with increasing demand the "price" for higher education has also increased, which is visible in the upward pressure on tuition fees especially in the US and the UK. This situation also puts new pressures towards the question of overall quality in higher education at large.

The new international if not (nearly) global market for higher education has only intensified the competition between the higher education institutions and between the countries, and even between the continents. In the "old" days the competition existed mostly within the universities, between the professors and between the students. The market is now entering a kind of academic capitalism where the competitive ability of higher education institutions seems to be moving towards visibility in research rather than in quality of teaching and learning as such. Certain "popular" international and national ranking lists often tend to strengthen this kind of "capitalism". This market situation, if not addressed properly, may eventually undermine some of the QA systems' value that is being built now for Europe, as part of the Bologna process. Thus the question remains: is a good position in some international league table more important than the certificate for the institution's QA system?

Namely, the new competitive situation may also distort the entire higher education field in the sense that it sometimes appears to rely more on commercial or publicity principles through the league tables or some other similar means rather than on the promotion of genuine public good. Instead of a provision of true information about the market situation on the quality of education, the end result may be very incomplete and confusing for decision-making by an individual student and the family. The higher education market may be very competitive, at least in outside appearance, but all the "customers" and stakeholders still may have but poor informational basis for rational decisions. The league tables may be based more on the reputation or "brand" construction of institutions rather than on their actual performance at the level of the individual student or learner. It may not be uncommon that some institutions would rather work on their market reputation than on the quality of the education they provide for their students. These issues have recently been discussed and analysed by Dill and Soo (2005).

But the overall conclusion should be that, with or without league tables, strong public guidance is needed in both the national and European policies and quality management at large in the higher education institutions if we wish to promote the true role of higher education in the production and advancement of human capital.

As a consequence of the new role of the universities and higher education at large in building human capital, the European higher education institutions in the last decades have been forced to open up, to become more transparent and responsible players in society. This is actually a world-wide development, and partly a consequence of the **ever larger share of each new age cohort entering higher education, and then the labour market.** The old actions and measures that were considered as having purely academic interests only through peer reviews are now open also to external scrutiny and criticism. The world outside the higher education institution now includes a large number of intertwined political, economic and social interests and pressures, which the higher education institution can no longer master in the same way that it used to handle its internal matters in the past, at least not through the old single-discipline and fragmented approach. This is a new challenge facing the management of the higher education institutions, and especially their leadership.

There is also strong pressure towards both national and international networking by the higher education institutions, which may seem contradictory in the competitive situation, but still it is seen as beneficial to the individual higher education institutions through their ability to concentrate on their main strengths and to draw on the best practices from outside. The networks may not necessarily be very stable and long-lasting, but a common framework of quality management could be, and to some extent already is, another bond to keep them together to the mutual benefit of all the partners. Enhanced mobility of both students and staff could greatly add to the stability of these networks. At its best a network could come close to a genuine win-win situation. In this context the concept of "quality" again becomes very dynamic and multidimensional, dependent on the context and the environment where each higher education institution functions. But, again, a shared concept of quality is needed and is actually necessary.

Thus the old concept of academic trust is being replaced by a new type of accountability, towards society at large, students, stakeholders and others. The old trust is still needed and is necessary also from the ethical point of view, but a more systematic means of assessing and evaluating is required. The QA system and its external assessment is one of them, though not necessarily the only one. In this sense the concept of accountability covers much more than just the position of a higher education institution in some league table.

In this very context, the role of the European QA systems as indicated in the standards and guidelines should assume a central role for the development of human capital in higher education, for the competitiveness and attractiveness of EHEA and Europe at large, and for the delivery of this very public good to its citizens and to the international higher education community at large. The somewhat generic nature of the standards and guidelines will in any case allow for national variations and interpretations of the QA systems, but the overall European framework should indeed be the basis for national QA structures and practices. But on the other hand, the expected role of higher education and the research potential are nationally seen as so crucial that the national higher education and innovation policies will still be the very undercurrent in the implementation of the QA systems. Yet in a way this should only strengthen the role of the European standards and guidelines. It is sometimes said that in the past the governments were supposed to provide for the universities, while now the universities (and polytechnics) are expected to provide for the governments. So the old cost-benefit ratio has been kind of turned upside-down.

* * *

In Finland, the Finnish Higher Education Evaluation Council (FINHEEC) has been embarking on a quality audit type of procedure in the evaluations of the QA systems, starting in 2005, and following the Berlin communiqué. This communiqué actually gives some leeway for the execution of the QA systems, which thus should include a "system of accreditation, certification or comparable procedures". A decision was made in 2004 to employ an audit system, but of course following the standards and guidelines. All Finnish higher education institutions are publicly financed, and all of them undergo annual "target" negotiations with the ministry, which has the power to decide which general academic fields are represented in each higher education institution. Thus the universities, for example, are already "accredited" by the parliament through the Universities Act. It is often stated that the audit procedure is better suited for the more mature higher education systems (for example Dill, 2000; Woodhouse, 2003). Currently, the higher education institutions are subject to many kinds of evaluations, including those covering their research activities, public services and more, and there thus may exist even a danger of evaluation "fatigue".

Each higher education institution in Finland can decide which type of quality system it wants to follow. It may be based on ISO standards, or on EFQM, or their modifications, or something else. The higher education institutions are also free to approach any national or international quality accreditation agencies or organisations, but only FINHEEC has national legal status as an evaluation agency for the higher education institutions. The legal mandate of FINHEEC only covers Finnish higher education institutions, not any foreign universities. In principle, the rectors will respond to the ministry of education concerning the results of their evaluations, in their annual contract negotiations. FINHEEC also performs thematic and programme evaluations as well as accreditations of higher education institutions'professional courses in addition to the quality audits. Currently and for the next few years the quality audits remain the main task of FINHEEC, though.

The audit criteria have been set in consultation with the higher education institutions in open and common seminars, and they are public. At first, there was a round of "pilot" audits in which the results and the experience obtained were carefully studied, and the detailed criteria and procedure were modified and developed further as need be. Each team of external auditors undergoes a period of intense training that in principle is the same regardless of the type of higher education institution being audited. The audit process involves site visits and the team also includes both student and labour market representatives. The audit report is published and dealt with in an open seminar, often with the media present.[6] Upon conclusion, FINHEEC will grant a quality certificate which is valid for six years, but if a higher education institution has apparent shortages or deficiencies in its QA system, the audit team nominated by FINHEEC will revisit the higher education institution in two years' time.

---

6. All audit reports are publicly available on FINHEEC's home page at www.finheec.fi.

The audit, as well as all other FINHEEC evaluations, are based on the overall principle of quality enhancement, which may also serve as a psychological "carrot" for the institutions. Right now (in 2006) virtually all Finnish higher education institutions have registered with FINHEEC to participate in the audit of their QA systems. Their apparent motivation is driven by the fact that they see it as an asset in the international higher education market, especially concerning student and staff mobility, or as a means of attracting foreign students, to say nothing of attracting talented and motivated students at large. Because the audit is based on a specific contract between the higher education institutions and FINHEEC, it is generally not seen as limiting the autonomy of the institutions. Yet, the autonomy in this sense is not without hidden problems; so far FINHEEC has paid for the cost of the external team and for its own secretarial work, but in the future there is pressure that each higher education institution should assume at least part of the cost. It may (or may not) lessen the interests of the higher education institutions to participate in the audit, and they may instead see it as more beneficial to look for other (international) QA audits or quality recognitions, unless future national policies define the situation in more detail. The Universities Act stipulates little to this effect, since the universities are only requested to evaluate their actions and the evaluations should be public. But so far, all Finnish higher education institutions are willing to participate in the audits. Of course, the autonomy of the higher education institutions is not absolute but they must follow the general direction of the national higher education and innovation policies. There is pressure to grant more financial autonomy to the Finnish universities, which is considered as a means of supporting their national and international competitiveness.

It is often stated as part of the Bologna process that the higher education institutions themselves are responsible for their own quality, also in reference to their autonomy. This gives the FINHEEC the principal role of a "helper" or that of a "liaison" towards each higher education institution. The higher education institution itself covers the costs of its self-evaluation (or its data-gathering) process, while other audit costs are covered by FINHEEC, as described above. The issue of the independence of the evaluation agency is also one of the key principles of the ENQA standards and guidelines. Accordingly, "infringing" upon the autonomy of the higher education institution is avoided by concluding a specific contract for the audit between FINHEEC and each higher education institution. It is important that the process aims also towards mutual trust-building through open and transparent process, so that the higher education institution really feels it can gain from the overall exercise by developing its QA activities following the audit. The results of the first audits have been very encouraging in this respect. If any problems have emerged, they are usually related to the relatively short period some higher education institutions have been developing their "quality culture"; such a culture that permeates the entire institution cannot be created in, say, one year alone. Another general observation is that in some cases the internal and the external evaluation do not fully meet each other, which may be related to certain "language" problems; the FINHEEC audit deals mostly with the processes, not with the outputs or similar performance indicators of the higher education institution.

The general issue of the legitimacy of the audit/accreditation process is still partially open, and this apparently applies throughout Europe. The national and regional evaluation agencies in Europe are usually covered by a specific law or decree, which gives them a nationally defined operational mandate. But in Finland it is the audit process itself which provides transparency, which is consistent and professionally performed by an independent agency, and which thus provides a necessary basis for its legitimacy. It is also important to continue building trust between the higher education institutions and the agency, which further enhances both legitimacy and accountability of the entire process. FINHEEC has recently issued a special Audit Manual[7] where the entire process including the aims, methods of assessment, the audit criteria, and the follow-up processes have been made publicly available.

As an obligation of their membership of ENQA, the QA agencies must undergo an external cyclical review periodically at least once every five years. The purpose is to assess whether the agencies meet the ENQA membership criteria but also the standards and guidelines for quality assurance endorsed by the European ministers in Bergen in 2005. A special European register of external QA agencies operating in Europe is in the making, under the umbrella of ENQA, EUA, EURASHE and ESIB, listing the agencies operating in Europe that are deemed "valid" and that fulfil the register's criteria, according to the planned categories of the register. The structure and management of this register are still open, but at least the general guidelines are expected to be ready for adoption at the ministers' meeting in London in May 2007.

The European higher education institutions live and work within a cultural, historical, administrative and legal diversity that may cause certain difficulties or even pitfalls in the implementation of the standards and guidelines for quality assurance. In principle, the situation is similar to that facing the European Union at large.

Recently (2006) the Nordic evaluation agencies, working together in the framework of the Nordic Quality Assurance Network in Higher Education (NOQA), finished a common project that analysed the situation concerning the applicability of the standards and guidelines, but from a Nordic perspective.[8] The Nordic agencies each have slightly different tasks, but in general they work under relatively similar legislation and cultural backgrounds.

Certain observations from this Nordic project may be useful in developing further the overall applicability of the European standards and guidelines. One of the major issues to be observed is that all quality assurance agencies naturally work in the context of their national higher education system, and within the national culture and traditions. The same applies to all higher education institutions as well. This needs to be mentioned here, though in Europe at large there is a common awareness of this "limitation", yet many could call it also an "asset".

---

7. www.finheec.fi/pdf/julkaisut/KKA_406.pdf.
8. www.noqa.net.

Accordingly, the Nordic project noted that it is necessary to produce more precise threshold values in relation to the standards and guidelines if the European agencies (and the higher education institutions) are to be reviewed in a consistent manner, and also respecting the national contexts and models at the same time. This has implications even down to the institutional level. The concept of European consistency may thus need further attention. Furthermore, the Nordic project noted that each agency has a set of informal practices ("tacit" knowledge) and arrangements which are not apparent in the written documents but which may nevertheless influence the outcome. Again, the same observation may apply to the assessment of every higher education institution as well.

A major obstacle in the application of the standards and guidelines may, however, be hidden in the language used. The standards contain a fairly complex terminology in English which it may not be possible to be translate and understand the same way in every country and every culture, even if the standards and guidelines were intended to function basically as generic reference points. Thus the legal documents and their terminology may prove to be insufficient as such in the consistent application of the procedures and methods. One pair of definitions that is often seen as confusing is "management" and "governance", while in fact the latter usually has a strong connotation of civil society. Actually, ENQA ran a workshop on "The Language of European Quality Assurance" in June 2006, where these problems were discussed at length. And, finally, the overall credibility of the reviewing process itself, be it targeted at the agencies or at the higher education institutions themselves, is not of secondary importance.

The Nordic project further discussed the issue of the official status of the agencies, that is, if they are a necessary part of the national quality assurance systems of higher education. In Finland, the higher education institutions can choose other agencies than FINHEEC for their quality assurance, but, at the same time, all higher education institutions are also participating in the quality audit of FINHEEC. The European register of the QA agencies that is in the planning may give the eligible agencies the possibility of working throughout the EHEA. Furthermore, the requirement for the independence of the agencies is a central issue for the credibility of the overall QA process: it may involve legal, administrative, financial, and operational independence.

The main message here may exist in the fact that legitimacy as such is a complex issue and may not depend merely on the actual legal status. Even more crucially, however, the QA process itself should be transparent, and coherent throughout Europe, and performed with credibility applying proper ethical standards to ensure also the rights of the institutions themselves.

But, at the end of the day, the main impetus for the legitimisation of QA systems is the Bologna Process itself, and the deep European commitment to it. Bologna is the European trademark for higher education, and it has also created a lot of interest far outside Europe. Thus a "stamp" of passing the European QA criteria should be an important factor for all European higher education institutions in the competitive and international higher education market. Of course, the Lisbon Recognition Convention is also an important pillar in building the EHEA, and it is simply strengthened by the European quality standards and related structures. This does not prevent the universities or polytechnics from obtaining other quality labels from other, professional or private sources, like EQUIS for the business schools, for instance. In this sense also we are moving towards the market orientation in QA in the higher education sector.

Needless to say, the leadership and governance of the higher education institution plays a crucial role in the creation and implementation of its QA system. This does not imply that the universities or polytechnics did not have any "quality" before this system, quite the contrary. It is important, however, that this system is based on a quality culture that concerns everybody in the institution. The leadership has to be the initiator of the strategic quality improvement in the institution, and the role of quality should then be further enhanced by the dissemination of good practice through national and international networks. Thus we can make the entire European higher education system a coherent one, and also a successful and competitive learning organisation that helps to build the human skills and human capital in the entire continent necessary for its cultural, financial and economic competitiveness.

References

Dill, D. D. (2000), "Designing academic audit: lessons learned in Europe and Asia", *Quality in Higher Education*, 6(3), pp. 187-207.

Dill, D. D. and Soo, M. (2005), "Academic quality, league tables, and public policy: a cross-national analysis of university ranking systems", *Higher Education*, 26(1), pp. 97-115.

ENQA, "Standards and guidelines for quality assurance in the European Higher Education Area". Adopted by the Bergen Conference of European ministers responsible for higher education, May 2005 (ISBN 952-5539-04-0).

Woodhouse, D. (2003), "Quality improvement through quality audit", *Quality in Higher Education*, 9(2), pp. 130-39.

The implications for governance of institutions and systems

Jürgen Kohler

1. The topic – approaches

Identifying and assessing roles, responsibilities, and means of public authorities in matters of quality assurance calls for an approach which categorises and segments, correlates and integrates, values and optimises all those elements constituting the given headline. So, this approach induces a basic pattern of analysis which applies the scheme: object – agent – action and objective. Using a more elaborative code, this translates into answering questions along the following itemisation: who does what, how, and why?; or else, looking at:

- the object: what is "quality assurance" as far as identifying concrete objects subjected to quality assurance is concerned? (2.);
- the agent: who are, or could be seen as, "public authorities"? (3.);
- the action and the objective: how, and why are roles, responsibilities, and means – *de facto* or optimally – attributed, shared, and used by public authorities? (4.).

Having dealt with these items, the context has been set in order to deal with the second challenge, that is, to consider:

- implications for governance of institutions and of systems

with regard to answers to these items (5.).

Owing to the fact that this article is intended to set the scene, it will indicate the relevant issues and suggest a feasible method of approach. It will not undertake to present answers in a ready-made way.

2. The object in focus: quality assurance

Quality assurance in higher education institutions is the object to consider. When leaving aside research activities here, this issue raises the question: assuring quality of exactly what, from which perspective, and with what consequence?

2.1. As for the "what" question, the issue is about identification of objects which are to be subjected to scrutiny. There is a multitude of choices. Quality assurance can, and often does in an additive way, focus on the following:

- staff: developing and selecting staff is a traditional approach, at least as old as Humboldt and his university, which brought about a serious dispute as to whether it was up to the university or the state to choose new academic teachers and researchers. In modern days this conflict still exists, but in some cases

its solution has been transferred to agencies, at least insofar as decisions on eligibility of candidates are concerned;
- programmes: there are two essentially different activities which can be related to the headline labelled "programme approach":
  - first, evaluating and accrediting the quality of concrete programmes offered by higher education institutions is a common feature of quality assurance in many systems. It is much favoured by professional bodies which assess programmes geared towards future would-be professionals. Beyond that programme assessment is viewed with some scepticism, mainly due to the costs accrued. All in all, there is scepticism in substance since this approach might stifle permanent quality enhancement within evaluation or accreditation periods and prevent higher education institutions from developing their own responsibilities for quality ambition and quality management by making them rather prone to wait-and-see attitudes and reliance on compliance-based policies of merely copying programme templates;
  - second, there is a more normative understanding of programme-based quality assurance with systems which provide a methodology for the development and proposal of model curricula for certain given academic fields. Here the programme approach to quality assurance is concerned with the ideal of templates and standardisation. There is a strong tendency to operate quality assurance on the notion of compliance, which may prevent institutions from developing profiles, from interdisciplinarity, and from free transfer of current research into up-to-date teaching and learning;
- institutions: this approach considers the entire operations of a given higher education institution. It is a complex matter covering educational and research activities as such, but also the legal, funding and administrative issues which shape and maintain the institution in all its facets;
- quality processes: looking at quality processes means taking that segment of the institutional approach which is linked to institutional operations designed to contribute to education, namely to developing, implementing, monitoring, and improving quality programmes. While assessing quality processes of a higher education institution can be described as an excerpt of the institutional approach, it can at the same time be seen as a meta-approach in relation to programme-based quality assurance since it views the circumstantial conditions which determine the quality of programmes provided as the result of planning, implementation and improvement activities;
- system assessment: system assessment considers the entire national or regional organisation of higher education as a provision made to serve the area in question best. This approach will usually encompass elements of the institutional approach but will go beyond this microlevel by addressing the overall optimisation of the system as a whole, that is, both its internal and societal interfaces, structures, and implications.

2.2. The "what" question may also be seen as covering matters of "perspective", that is by the viewpoint from which the issues mentioned above are seen, and to what end, and which interests are to be served. In that respect, there may be three different aspects:

- first, whose perspective is being sought. This indicates mainly the difference between in-house appraisal and external assessment. Both approaches can be applied to all of the five different objects of quality assurance mentioned above;
- second, there can be differences as to consequences of quality assurance. Quality assurance can be advisory, as is usually the case with mere evaluations. However, if evaluations take on an element of certification to be used externally for reasons of funding or of advertising, or even a legal function in the sense of permission or licensing to operate a particular activity, quality assurance can be much more invasive and more or less prescriptive;
- eventually, there is a need to consider the interests of various participants, or stakeholders, in higher education concerning specific features and characteristics which they, from their particular perspective and needs, consider to be essential elements of quality and would therefore like to be covered by quality assurance. Looking at providers and recipients, who nevertheless are interacting partners at the same time, a survey of those involved and their vested interests may look like this:

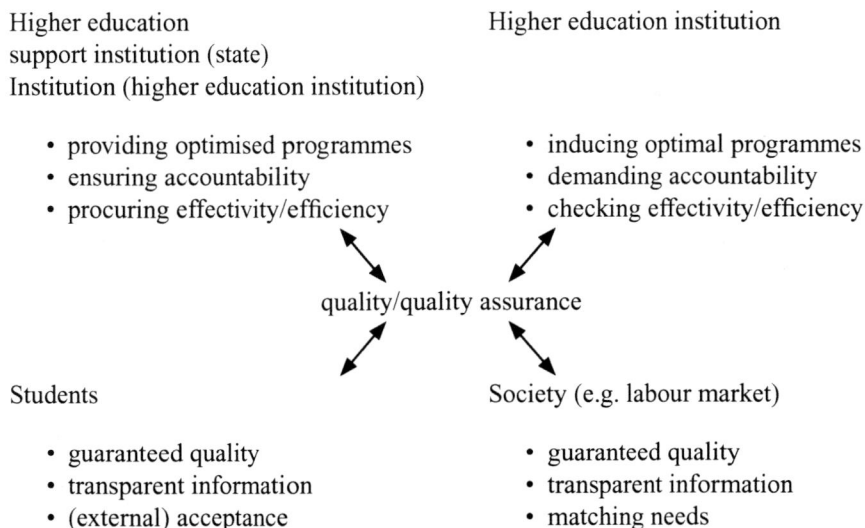

Higher education
support institution (state)
Institution (higher education institution)

Higher education institution

- providing optimised programmes
- ensuring accountability
- procuring effectivity/efficiency

- inducing optimal programmes
- demanding accountability
- checking effectivity/efficiency

quality/quality assurance

Students

- guaranteed quality
- transparent information
- (external) acceptance

Society (e.g. labour market)

- guaranteed quality
- transparent information
- matching needs

3. The agent: public authorities – identification

Identifying "public authorities" as agents in quality assurance seems to be a straightforward matter. It certainly includes states, as represented by ministries charged with higher education and research. However, it is suggested that there could be a wider notion of "public authorities", which could, all in all and perhaps to some surprise or doubt, comprise the following institutions:

- higher education institutions;
- nation state(s)/national ministries;
- international public organisations;
- quality assurance agency(ies);
- professional organisations.

3.1. Higher education institutions certainly are agents in matters of quality assurance. Ever since at least the Berlin Communiqué there has been an explicit understanding across Europe that it is they who bear prime responsibility for quality of higher education offers, and for quality assurance as well. And yet, there may be some doubt as to whether higher education institutions are public authorities in the sense used here. However, leaving aside the issue of private higher education institutions, it is true in a formal sense that they are bodies established by public law endowed with institutional and operational rights and duties immediately derived from, and vested in, public authority derived from legislation and serving the public good. In substance, it is correct and inevitable to count them as public authorities in this context since their absence would ignore both their significance in steering the quality system as a whole and their vested obligation and prerogative to do so delegated to them by virtue of state authority.

3.2. It is self-evident that the nation state is a relevant public authority. However, even here things can get complex wherever there are federal systems of various kinds in place. Still, this item is easily seen; by contrast, the other agents will need some explanation and justification.

3.3. International public organisations may at first glance not be seen as self-evident "public authorities" in the realm of quality assurance. However, institutions such as the European Union and the Council of Europe are undoubtedly public authorities; the question comes down to whether they act as such in matters of quality assurance. Indeed, they do so, either in terms of law or *de facto*.

As for legal involvement in quality assurance, for example, even cases such as the Lisbon Recognition Convention promoted by the Council of Europe impacts on quality assurance. The question whether or not qualifications are recognised across borders is intrinsically linked to guarded trust in the quality of programmes provided by the higher education system the qualifications of which are to be recognised, and so recognition practice will have to take into consideration – or, to say the least, it will indirectly promulgate – how developed a quality assurance system of countries party to the convention is.

More subtly, there is tremendous *de facto* influence on quality and quality assurance issues exercised by certain activities and approaches of the European Union. This pertains to undertakings to draft a number of "Euro-models", for example the "Eurochemist" or the "Euro-engineer" or the like. These activities indicate that there will be pan-European programmatic reference points of considerable significance since inertia will work towards using them as templates and applying them in quality assurance processes as yardsticks, asking for compliance as the "simple way to quality".

Furthermore, and not least, the Bologna Process might be considered as a "public authority" in the wider sense. Although – or possibly because – it is not a formally recognised operation leading to legal instruments under international law, it is an activity operated jointly by public authorities which work out common policies and instruments. In doing so, the process has emerged to produce considerable impact as a means of orientation, calibration, validation, and a general reference point for numerous matters of quality in higher education. To name just the essential ones, the European Qualifications Framework – which defines the entire system of the European higher education area with *de facto* binding effect for member states, including the descriptor system and ECTS as well as the essential shifts from teaching to learning and from input to outcomes orientation – and the standards and guidelines for quality assurance lead the way towards developing, implementing, and assessing matters of quality authoritatively.

3.4. As for quality assurance agencies, these are – at least whenever they wield power to the extent that their decisions are more or less essential for operating academic programmes, as may be the case in systems based on accreditation – "public authorities" because they operate on the basis of authority delegated by their nation state – or by higher education institutions – thus exercising legal and economic authority on behalf of that country and its democratic institutions. This is clearly indicated by the fact that agencies, their duties and rights are established by national legislation or some type of ministerial decree, and that these duties and rights are vested in them as agents operating in lieu of the state or of higher education institutions which would otherwise act itself or, respectively, themselves in the area of quality assurance. This is also why decisions made by these agencies are – or at least should be – subject to the rule of law and judicial review.

However, there is a specific difference as compared to direct state intervention and role. Quality assurance agencies are "buffer organisations" in several aspects, which follows directly from the standards and guidelines as accepted by the Bergen communiqué. First, they should act independent of state operations, though subject to the rule of law. Second, they should include peer involvement, which is an element of self-governance of those concerned. In that respect, it may be fair to say that the establishment of, and the role attributed to, quality assurance agencies is part of states' policies to accept and even to promulgate activities of what has become known as "civil society".

When having a brief look at research, it may also be said that national, or self-governing, research councils serve as quality assurance agencies. They judge quality by making judgments on the quality of proposed research programmes on behalf of the budget provider, which is, by and large, the state. In that wider sense of administering public functions under public authority, they could also be seen as "public institutions".

3.5. Finally, taking up the notion of "civil society" and carrying it further, professional organisations should be counted among "public authorities". This may be arguable, since indeed these are not necessarily public entities. However, to some extent they are, and they may accurately be identified as public–private partnerships. These agents, such as law societies, medical, veterinary or pharmaceutical associations, or engineering bodies in some countries, enjoy the authority to define programme standards – be it by virtue of specific legal instruments under national law, by virtue of tradition or just by *de facto* dominance of the specific labour market sector. Any such authority in "regulated professions" is of utmost significance, partly in a legal sense and partly *de facto*, for higher education institutions, either directly or via accreditation. This would not be the case if national authorities did not permit this to happen, and that is why it may be said that this set-up is another example of devolving state, that is, public, authority to a "buffer organisation" embedded into certain spheres of the civil domain.

3.6. An overview summarising the relevant agents may look like this:

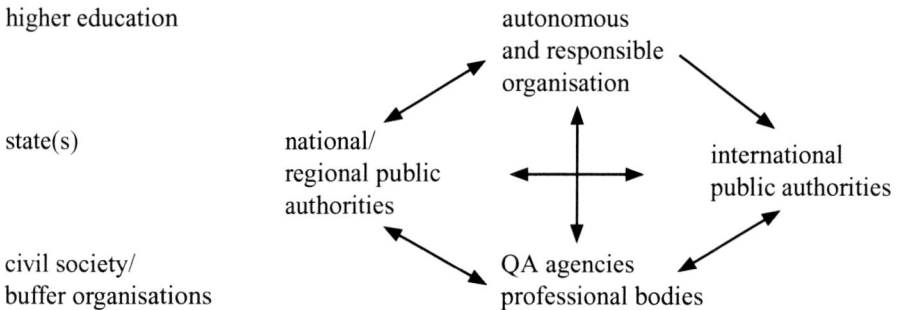

higher education

autonomous
and responsible
organisation

state(s)

national/
regional public
authorities

international
public authorities

civil society/
buffer organisations

QA agencies
professional bodies

4. Objectives and action: roles, responsibilities and means

4.1. Asking for roles, responsibilities and means provokes drafting organisational charts and diagrams, and also provokes sketching workflow sheets. There is a point in doing this; but it is not the starting point. These items are results, but not the initial concern. They cannot be the foremost item because they require orientation – a yardstick – in order to be able to answer the question: why should this particular organisational set-up be chosen or be preferable to others?

4.2. Instead, it is crucial to realise that the well-known Bauhaus maxim for good architecture applies to identifying apt attribution of roles, responsibilities, and means in higher education organisations as well, which is: form follows function. So, what are higher education functions, that is, ulterior purposes? In concrete terms, as far as quality assurance is concerned: what is understood by "good quality" in higher education, or research, or service to society as an overriding concept?

4.2.1. So, from an overall point of view, the guideline of institutional quality, and also the guideline for public authorities in safeguarding quality in higher education institutions, is "fitness for purpose" ("purposefulness"). Aims and mission are key indicators to governance and management issues, and these aims and mission are:

- to be productive in research and learning and to enhance quality and quantity in these fields;
- to support individual students' personal development;
- to aim at meeting cultural needs and international, national, or regional advancement of society (namely, by fostering "democratic citizenship"), also in economic terms (mainly, by securing "employability").

On this background, higher education institutions are instruments for meeting these objectives. Their quality is defined by the quality of the outcome mentioned above which results from their operations supported and encouraged by a suitable institutional framework. So, institutional governance and management, as well as any quality assurance approach by public authorities, must ensure that there is, and will be, such quality of outcome to the highest degree possible, achieved at a minimum of administrative, financial, and "political" waste and delay.

These questions and challenges, that is, the points to raise in order to arrive at maximum quality by means of optimal organisational devices, will be considered hereafter. This will here be done by limiting the aspect to matters of quality assurance with specific focus on matters of teaching and learning, thus not addressing more closely aspects of research or knowledge transfer into society.

4.2.2. Quality (of teaching and learning) is the key feature of orientation. However, quality is an ambiguous concept. Here are some proposals:

- excellence;
- fitness of and for purpose;
- matching directives (complying with curricular templates);
- meeting thresholds (complying with standards);
- client/customer satisfaction;
- value for money/time invested (efficiency);
- individual enhancement (transformation);
- (institutional) capacity for change.

It is obvious that the choice between the quality concepts listed here is of paramount significance to governance and management choices in systems. For instance, where there is a "compliance" approach, in essence matters of design are located outside higher education institutions – ministries, or expert teams of various kinds – and while these bodies are entrusted with matters of concept, higher education institutions will only be asked to implement truthfully. This results in a concept of merely executionary functions, which consists of implementation management and monitoring. On the other hand, where there is an open concept of quality, as is the case in a fitness of and for purpose approach, there needs to be an entrepreneurial style of governance and management which first of all identifies future opportunities and threats based on sound analysis of present-day strengths and weaknesses, scrutiny of societal environment and means, and then transforms such analysis into profiled concepts which are then implemented, monitored, and improved again and again.

Putting just these two concepts side by side in a graph clearly indicates that the challenge posed to establishing a "good quality system" heavily depends on the concept of quality adopted.

A "compliance-based approach" is, in principle, rather simple; it may look like this:

Model template (t): features $a(t) + b(t) + c(t) + \ldots + z(t)$

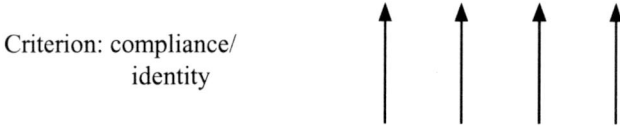

Criterion: compliance/
        identity

$\uparrow \quad \uparrow \quad \uparrow \quad \uparrow$

Concrete programme (p): features $a(p) + b(p) + c(p) + \ldots + z(p)$

It does not ask for much competence at the level of higher education institutions, nor does it ask for much at the level of external quality assurance agencies. However, it is highly complex when it comes to defining centralised authorities and the level of governments or particular agencies set up for developing any such reference templates or standards, and this is true both for matters of institutional legitimacy and for aptness of their concrete operations and decisions.

On the other hand, a "fitness of and for purpose approach" is a much more open concept. It may be illustrated as follows by depicting what is aptly known as the "quality cycle", or rather, the "quality spiral":

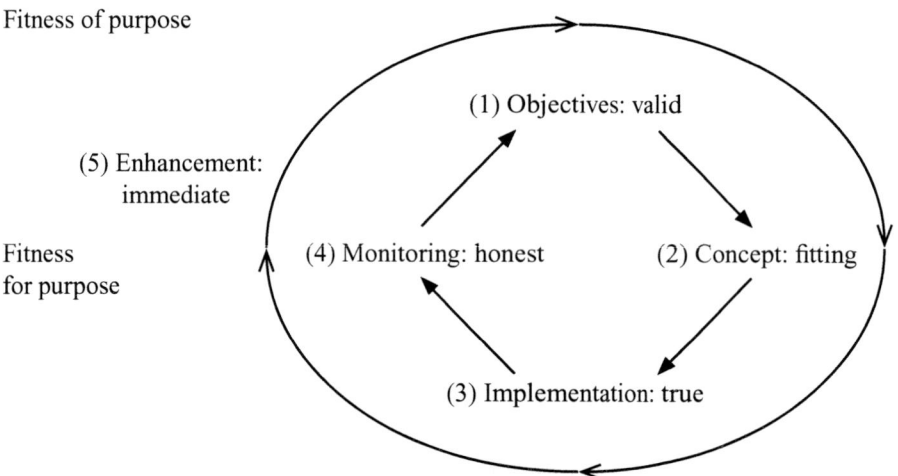

Fitness of purpose

(5) Enhancement:
    immediate

(1) Objectives: valid

Fitness
for purpose

(4) Monitoring: honest

(2) Concept: fitting

(3) Implementation: true

Any such more complex notion of quality requires more complex structures of governance and management at the level of higher education institutions. This is the point where institutional challenges to mastering true autonomy begin. These challenges encompass the ability of an institution, by means of its quality culture, its governance and its managerial operations, to steer the "quality cycle" effectively and efficiently to utmost satisfaction.

At this point, at the latest, the link between the "issue of programme quality", as a matter of institutional "function", and the "issue of institutional quality", as a matter of form, becomes transparent. To be more precise, the link between the purposes of education and institutional set-up in terms of governance, management and culture is made via the ability of the institution to steer those processes which constitute the quality cycle autonomously, effectively, and efficiently. This link could be put into the following diagram:

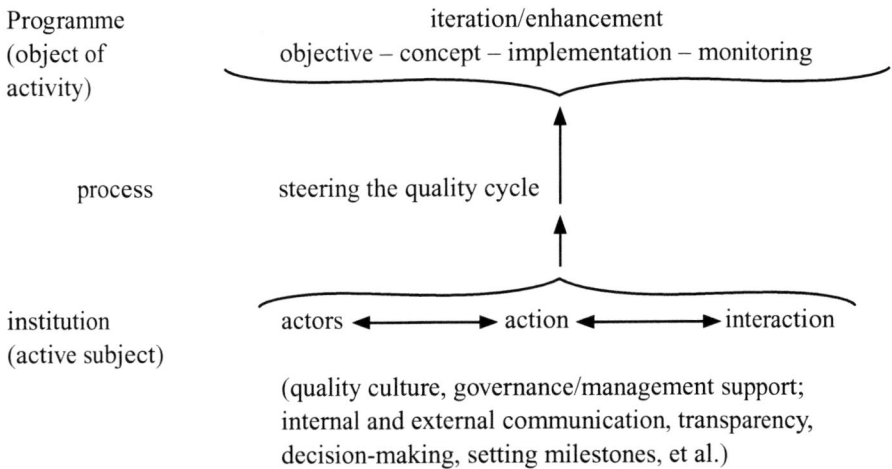

Programme   iteration/enhancement
(object of   objective – concept – implementation – monitoring
activity)

process   steering the quality cycle

institution   actors ←⟶ action ←⟶ interaction
(active subject)

(quality culture, governance/management support;
internal and external communication, transparency,
decision-making, setting milestones, et al.)

If this is a concept of quality which shapes the concept of quality management, it lays open the close dependence of programme-related quality on governance and management matters. The key understanding is: programme quality is ensured best by steering the institutional process optimally along the line of the quality cycle; that is by shaping and organising institutional culture and management – with all its facets of actors, action, and interaction – by asking which institutional set-up, devices, processes render substantial results when considering each item along the line which constitutes and safeguards quality of study programmes.

However, this connection influences external quality assurance as well. As a consequence, its task is focused on supporting and assessing whether or not the process described above is established, both by concept and in reality. Good governance of systems is indicated by the extent to which this is accomplished, and moreover, to what extent it applies the very same concept to its own operations.

4.3. Another element of basic orientation must be borne in mind: what are the corollaries, namely the circumstantial features in which higher education is embedded, and of the people involved in higher education? Mechanistic approaches to roles, responsibilities, means of public authorities, as well as to governance principles, will fail and be detrimental if they do not take heed of cultural circumstances, including the very essence of research and research-based teaching and learning, and of the type of people involved in any such activity. The following items may be recalled here, which are prerequisites defined by, and consequences deriving from, purpose and people inside the system and society outside the system:

- freedom of research and teaching/learning: this is not only a right pertaining to the individual; it is a prerequisite for progress and innovation since it is essential to move the frontiers of knowledge and to ensure dynamic evolution rather than promulgate static concepts of passing on traditional acquired expertise only. Freedom of teaching, learning, and research encompasses, within the limits of ethics, the freedom to choose subject, hypothesis, and methodology, thus safeguarding that "the unexpected can be expected"; as a consequence, there is a limit to the expedience of managed planification approaches to higher education and research;
- freedom of research and learning attracts, and needs, free individuals whose integration into a team is a major challenge;
- change of paradigm towards the "entrepreneurial university" facing national or international competition subject to transnational educational frameworks and mobility;
- increasing costs (staff, equipment, media, buildings, etc.) and advanced communication technology, cheap transport, internationalisation of standards, increasing mobility, programmes provided globally could lead to concerted structures (franchising systems, "chain-stores" and "trusts");
- increasing awareness of the difference between legitimacy to be involved (*de jure* competence) and ability to be involved (*de facto* competence) – also pertaining to role-sharing between government level and "performance level" at higher education institutions;
- not only politics in the traditional sense, but also society as such may define themselves as stakeholders who seek influence.

5. Implications for governance of institutions and systems – outlining a methodology of items and questions to consider

Translating the aforementioned orientations and circumstantial opportunities, which may also be seen as limits, into governance matters at institutional and systems level cannot be done by developing a blueprint which serves as a ready-made for everyone. This is prevented by the fact that institutions and systems vary not only in size, which brings about different constraints and opportunities, but also with regard to mission, tradition, legal and economic frameworks, and mentalities.

Therefore, at this stage governance issues can only be tackled by identifying the points to consider. These may be a matter of considering conflicting, or rather integrating, aspects, which must eventually be brought into an integral concept.

Items to:

- consider;
- explore;
- define;
- correlate;
- translate into governance and management structures;
- integrate into synergetic forces;
- test-run;

that is, the action to be carried out – following the sequencing as itemised above – in order to arrive at valid answers as to developing a quality system of governance and management of higher education institutions and systems, could be the following. These are broken down into two major categories:

- basic and overriding points of orientation;
- concrete operational challenges: functions, actors, action, and interaction.

These items should, first of all but not exclusively, be applied to higher education institutions, and then to systems steering as well. This prioritisation follows from the fact that higher education institutions are to enjoy autonomy, and that their autonomy should lead them to accept prime responsibility for the quality of their operations; this, at least for teaching and learning, is the overriding principle as expressed in various communiqués of the Bologna Process. Hence higher education institutions should primarily meet demands on governance and management required to match their institutional roles and responsibilities so assigned.

5.1. The following basic and overriding points of orientation, may be considered – and it is at this point where the issue links up with those points considered above as regards roles, responsibilities, and means:

- in substance: key orientation of judgment on organisational quality, to be based on aptness:
  - to identify valid aims ("fitness of purpose"); and
  - to achieve them by suitable means ("fitness for purpose");
  - while distinguishing between strategic dimension ("capacity for change [for the better]") and managerial operations; and
  - while observing "embeddedness": societal expectations, legal framework, funding, mentalities of partners, stakeholders, employees;

– in maxims: governance based on, and supporting:
  • motivation rather than external control ("ownership");
  • transcending from managerial mechanisms to spirit ("quality culture");
  • blending of leadership and responsiveness to staff incentives ("bottom-up, top-down");
  • self-balanced system rather than permanent intervention;
  • responsibility (rights) and accountability (liability) inseparable;
  • values, for example observing ethics and education for democratic citizenship;
  • permanence of review and updating (move from quality assurance to quality enhancement);
  • effectiveness and (cost-)efficiency.

These maxims may need to be explained in the context of the aforementioned key orientation of any quality judgment on organisational matters of higher education institutions or systems.

Steering devices of a higher education institution and indeed the entire system must be gauged against its purposefulness as to the ability of the system, that is, its organisation and its proceedings, to meet the aims defined above. Within this overall approach, it is sound policy to ensure minimising waste within the system ("efficiency"); this encompasses optimising procedures (effectiveness of cost and time). It is part of such policy to ensure that a self-steering, intrinsically stabilised and intrinsically mobilised system is developed; that is, a system consisting of elements which are designed, composed and arranged to form a system within which all people and all institutional elements interact as much as possible to bring about and achieve the aims mentioned above. Evidently, this encompasses the need to strengthen the self-motivation of those to be involved. Again, it follows from this maxim that managerial tasks, responsibility and accountability, and handling finances must be concentrated in the hands of those people and at various institutional levels which carry out the job in question, while making sure there is no wasteful doubling of operations.

– in process: transparency and integration, that is:
  • monitoring of and reporting on activities;
  • internal and external communication and responsiveness;

– in organisational clarity: defining structures, organs, actors, action in terms of
  • creation;
  • selection and election;
  • attribution of rights and duties;
  • interfaces and interaction;
  • responsibility, accountability, and liability;
  • cancellation, revocation;

- itemisation drafted above to be concretely applied to all fields of activities; that is:
  - study programmes (existence and design/contents);
  - research (current projects, and strategic development);
  - knowledge transfer (service to society; co-operative activities);
  - quality management;
  - financing (income sources, allocation, expenditure);
  - staffing (in particular senior staff – professors and top management);
  - communication (internal; external).

5.2. With regard to operational challenges – or rather, choices – relating to concrete functions, actors, action, and interaction, the following items should be explored:

- internality and externality:
  - roles and functions of state and of higher education institution;
  - roles of civil society (namely, role of boards);
  - in particular: role of (other) "buffer organisations", for example quality assurance agencies;
  - safeguarding responsiveness to society (for example, the labour market);

- leadership, integration, and the individual:
  - consultation;
  - participation;
  - co-operation;
  - checks and balances;
  - freedom and integration of the individual;

- centralisation and devolution:
  - international bodies/state/higher education institution;
  - head office/faculty-department/flexible ("project") structures;
  - individual;

- choice of steering and learning devices:
  - legalistic/normative standards: regulation and contract management;
  - economic/funding: distributive and/or competitive success, reward systems;
  - communicative: feedback, creating conviction, rallying support;
  - expertise: substantial competence;
  - responsibility: personal ownership and liability;
  - political: external values and directives given.

5.3. It may be assumed that the itemisation presented here pertains to higher education institutions only. However, this would be doubly wrong. First of all, at systems level the very same questions will have to be asked in order to optimise governance and management of any such system as such. Moreover, as far as there is a responsibility at systems level to ensure that the quality of its higher education institution is assured, safeguarded, and enhanced it is indispensable at system level to know how to approach the organisational quality issue at the level of higher education institutions. For if such expertise and methodology is not applied, there will be no sound yardstick as to judging established or projected governance or managerial matters inside the organisations of higher education of that system. This is a clear indicator of the coincidence and convergence of governance issues at systems and at higher education institutional level under the auspices, and with regard to, the overriding common denominator: to serve society through teaching and learning, research and knowledge transfer, as well as possible, that is by providing "good" quality within the mission of higher education.

Quality assurance
in the European Higher
Education Area

Implementation of the guidelines adopted
by the European ministers responsible for higher education

Peter Williams

In September 2003, the ministers of education of the European Higher Education Area (EHEA) gathered in Berlin for their biennial meeting and signed a communiqué which included the following sentence: "At the European level, Ministers call upon ENQA through its members, in co-operation with the EUA, EURASHE and ESIB, to develop an agreed set of standards, procedures and guidelines on quality assurance, to explore ways of ensuring an adequate peer review system for quality assurance and/or accreditation agencies or bodies, and to report back through the Follow-up Group to Ministers in 2005." This came as a surprise to ENQA, which had not been consulted about the proposal. The communiqué gave no indication of the intended purpose of such standards, procedures and guidelines, how they were to be used, or, indeed, what was meant by the phrase itself. Nevertheless, over the next eighteen months ENQA, EUA, ESIB and EURASHE came together to form the so-called "E4 Group" and worked hard to devise a European dimension to quality assurance which would meet the ministers' call.

Two working groups were set up by ENQA. One worked on the peer review system for agencies. This drew heavily on ENQA's own membership approval procedures and produced a model review process which would provide a robust, independent, assessment of agencies. The second working group set about devising standards and guidelines for institutions' and agencies' quality assurance processes.

Any pan-European set of standards would have to meet some tough criteria. They would need to be acceptable to all EHEA signatories; respect national and regional autonomy over higher education; recognise the very great differences in traditions, approaches and expectations among the higher education systems of Europe; and yet say something useful about quality assurance which all (or most) could accept as representing sound principles and good practice. This did not prove to be an easy task. An overriding need to reflect the principle of subsidiarity in European practices led the working group to drop "procedures" from the "standards, procedures and guidelines", because procedures would have been descriptions of "how" the standards should be met, and that would have encroached on local arrangements and responsibilities.

Eventually the two working groups produced a single unified report, which the E4 Group endorsed and forwarded to the 2005 ministerial meeting in Bergen. The report proposed not only standards and guidelines for quality assurance, but also a register of assurance and accreditation agencies operating in Europe and a quality assurance forum covering the interests of a wide range of stakeholders. The ministers adopted the standards and guidelines and these now stand as the key reference points for quality assurance across the EHEA.[9] The E4 Group was also asked to examine the practicalities of a register and report back to the next ministerial meeting, in London in 2007.

One of the main problems facing the working groups was the basic definition and purpose of the very words "quality assurance", "standards" and "guidelines". These are all generic terms with many interpretations across Europe (and more widely). Because of this, the group had to make a decision not to define quality assurance or the other terms arbitrarily, in ways that would be understood or recognised in only some parts of the EHEA, but instead to identify principles and values which it hoped would find acceptance as representing an authentic and truly European approach to the way in which good higher education is provided (and guaranteed).

Underpinning the standards and guidelines are three fundamental principles: the interests of students, employers, and society more generally, in good quality higher education; the central importance of institutional autonomy, tempered by a recognition that this brings with it heavy responsibilities; and the need for a "fitness for purpose" test for external quality assurance, which ensures that the burden that it places on institutions is no greater than is absolutely necessary.

The standards and guidelines are also dependent upon a series of general assumptions about European higher education, which follow to a large extent the spirit of the EUA's Graz Declaration of 2003: "the purpose of a European dimension to quality assurance is to promote mutual trust and improve transparency while respecting the diversity of national contexts and subject areas". These assumptions are as follows:

- providers of higher education have the primary responsibility for the quality of their provision and its assurance;
- the interests of society in the quality and standards of higher education need to be safeguarded;
- the quality of academic programmes needs to be developed and improved for students and other beneficiaries of higher education across the EHEA;
- there need to be efficient and effective organisational structures within which those academic programmes can be provided and supported;
- transparency and the use of external expertise in quality assurance processes are important;
- there should be encouragement of a culture of quality within higher education institutions;
- processes should be developed through which higher education institutions can demonstrate their accountability, including accountability for the investment of public and private money;
- quality assurance for accountability purposes is fully compatible with quality assurance for enhancement purposes;

---

9. Standards and Guidelines for Quality Assurance in Higher Education, ENQA, Helsinki, 2005; see www.enqa.eu/files/ENQA%20Bergen%20Report.pdf.

- institutions should be able to demonstrate their quality at home and internationally;
- processes used should not stifle diversity and innovation.

For their part, the standards and guidelines themselves are intended to encourage the development of higher education institutions which foster vibrant intellectual and educational achievement; provide a source of assistance and guidance to higher education institutions and other relevant agencies in developing their own culture of quality assurance; inform and raise the expectations of higher education institutions, students, employers and other stakeholders about the processes and outcomes of higher education; and contribute to a common frame of reference for the provision of higher education and the assurance of quality within the EHEA.

The European standards and guidelines comprise 23 standards grouped into three sections. Seven cover institutions' internal quality assurance, eight cover external quality assurance processes, and eight cover the quality assurance of agencies themselves. The internal quality assurance standards state principles of good practice relating to different aspects of academic activity; the external quality assurance standards are concerned with agencies' review activities; and the final group is designed to establish the constitutional and operational basis of trustworthy and credible agencies. For each standard there are guidelines, which explain the individual standards and offer illustrations of good practice.

As important as the standards and guidelines themselves, though regrettably rarely mentioned, is the commentary in the ENQA report on them and their intended uses. This highlights the danger of using the standards simplistically as a checklist; the importance of steady evolution and development of institutional and national quality assurance systems, rather than the imposition of "compliance" requirements; and the inappropriateness of trying to turn the standards and guidelines into the basis of a standardised European quality assurance system. So, for example, the report makes clear that:

> "The EHEA operates on the basis of individual national responsibility for higher education and this implies autonomy in matters of external quality assurance. Because of this the report is not and cannot be regulatory but makes its recommendations and proposals in a spirit of mutual respect among professionals; experts drawn from higher education institutions including students; ministries; and quality assurance agencies. Some signatory states may want to enshrine the standards and review process in their legislative or administrative frameworks. Others may wish to take a longer view of the appropriateness of doing so, weighing the advantages of change against the strengths of the status quo."

Unfortunately, the intention that the standards and guidelines should be viewed and used as common reference points in the context of national and regional subsidiarity, appear to have been ignored in some countries. Several have indeed enshrined the standards and guidelines into their national legislation, with a mandatory requirement that they be implemented, but some may have done so without due reflection on whether this was the most appropriate response to the real challenge that the standards and guidelines present. In these cases the standards are being used as statements of obligation, rather than as reference points to guide institutions and agencies as they move forward on what, for many, will inevitably be a very long journey. As a result, the true value of the standards and guidelines, as a formative and developmental tool, is less likely to be realised.

There is a further problem. The European standards and guidelines have also been proposed as the criteria for entry into the envisaged register of European quality assurance agencies and this is likely to bring with it a call for revisions to make them more easily usable for that particular purpose. Inevitably, if this happens, the standards and guidelines will slip towards the checklist of compliance requirements which the authors were at such pains to avoid.

Does this matter? Isn't it right that progress in quality assurance should be speeded up, if necessary by mandatory requirements? There is here a balance to be struck. Quality assurance remains a very contested area of both policy and practice, and there are only a very few countries in which the words are not greeted with a shudder of fear or hostility by the academic community. The concept has too frequently been presented simply as a form of burdensome external inspection, perceived by higher education as undermining its academic freedom in the name of consumer protection, or demanding compliance as a way of guaranteeing ultimate public control of universities, as a trade-off for increased notional autonomy. But there is another version of quality assurance, one which places at its centre the professionalisation of teaching and the conscious organisation of learning, which emphasises the need for careful effort to make sure that students are offered the best opportunities possible to achieve their full potential as learners. This version of quality assurance focuses on student and teacher, on the clarity of educational purpose and the means of meeting it, and on the collective endeavours of all who are involved in teaching and learning. It downplays the idea of quality assurance as a regulatory tool and instead emphasises its developmental value and practical usefulness.

One of the lessons that the past ten years have taught us is that quality assurance in higher education is most effective when it is owned by the individuals and institutions that are providing the learning opportunities for students. Only academics and institutions can truly assure quality, and it is much better if they are encouraged to take that responsibility upon themselves, as part of their professional role, rather than being dictated to by external controllers. Legislative imposition of the European standards and guidelines, although offering a highly visible indication of national commitment, may not always help the improvement of the quality of higher education.

We must be alert to this danger and do our best to avert it. How can we do this? First by trying to create and then consolidate the idea of quality as an intrinsic thread in an institution's academic life. The EUA has done groundbreaking work in its Quality

Culture Project, and it is now necessary to analyse the lessons learnt from that exercise and develop ways of broadening, deepening and embedding across the EHEA the good practice that has been identified.

Secondly, there is an educational task to be undertaken to help policymakers at government level to recognise the value of alternative models of quality assurance to those which rely on blind compliance with externally imposed requirements. The public interest in Europe may be best served by strong, autonomous higher education institutions which recognise and respond constructively to the serious public responsibility they hold, and which equally accept the benefit and value – to them as well as to others with a direct or indirect interest – of external reviews of their work. This is not to belittle the accountability function of quality assurance, which remains centrally important, but to advocate that the maximum benefit will probably be extracted from activities that cost a lot of time and money and which, if not carefully managed, can divert too many resources from the central purposes of higher education institutions.

Third, quality assurance and accreditation agencies should use their pivotal position between institutions, funders, governments and the public to promote and foster a wider and clearer understanding of quality in higher education. Everyone wants "good quality", but few can identify it or give a coherent account of its characteristics. "We know it when we see it" is not a sufficient response to the question "What is quality"? The agencies have a duty to answer that question more helpfully.

Finally, there needs to be a wide discussion of the European standards and guidelines themselves, to see how far the assumptions underpinning them are truly shared and do truly represent the values and principles of European higher education, as understood by practitioners in higher education institutions, students, governments, employers and others. Only dialogue will ensure the proper development of the ideas contained in the standards and guidelines, and this will be a long and, at times, possibly confusing debate. It is important that this, their principal purpose and value, is not diluted or diminished by an over-enthusiasm to use them as a checklist with no other intention than to ensure that the boxes can be ticked.

The European standards and guidelines are still new and will take some time to be understood and their usefulness fully discovered. Despite this there is already considerable evidence that they are being seen as making a serious contribution to the work of higher education institutions in the EHEA countries. The text has been translated into a number of languages (which itself has given rise to a number of questions relating to the meaning of some of the key words) and they are the subject of debate and discussion in many conferences and seminars. This is good, so long as they do not become the starting point for a standardised European quality assurance system, but do meet their objective of helping towards a wider understanding across the EHEA of the importance of quality in higher education, and offering shared lines of enquiry and action to assure and improve it.

The Bulgarian approach

Patricia Georgieva

1. Background

In 1997 accreditation was implemented in Bulgaria as a means of external peer review for accountability and quality improvement of all types of higher education institutions and programmes.

For nearly a decade accreditation in Bulgaria was legally defined as recognition by an authorised body of compliance with the law and the state requirements.[10] The term "quality" in that period was rarely mentioned in legal documents and then only to legitimise accreditation as something that stimulates institutions to improve their quality. In effect, the evaluation reports and accreditation decisions of the agency constituted accounts of compliance to legal requirements, but very little was said about the quality and academic standards in the courses and programmes offered by the respective institution. Considering agency reports as descriptions of how well public money is spent on higher education, it remains doubtful whether it is in the interest of the taxpayers to be periodically assured that universities abide by the law and adhere to state requirements, externally imposed on them. Perhaps it would be more relevant to inform the stakeholders whether students in Bulgarian universities acquire knowledge and skills comparable to that of their European coevals and whether the qualifications they obtain will help them to find a place in the job market?

2. The new quality assurance setting

2.1. Legal provisions

In an attempt to overcome these inconsistencies, the 2004 legal provisions define accreditation as the recognition of degree awarding powers of the institutions on the ground of an evaluation of the quality of their provision. Compared to the 1999 legal definition, the new text marks the shift from evaluation of compliance to evaluation

---

10. The initial period between 1996 and 1999 was dominated by the publicly accepted need for an external measure of quality and control over the standards of programmes and awards that Bulgarian institutions offer their students. To this end, the Ministry of Education and Science initiated and co-ordinated in 1994 a process of design of uniform state requirements for each programme of study. By 1998 nearly 200 study programmes had been provided with state requirements, approved by the government as individual legal acts. The first task of the newly established (by a government decree, in August 1996) National Evaluation and Accreditation Agency was to check the compliance of programmes with the uniform state requirements. The process ended in 2002, when a government decree abolished programme-by-programme state requirements and replaced them with a national qualifications framework. By that time the agency was also gaining experience in institutional evaluation and accreditation, yet again led by the perception of quality assurance as process and procedures for checking compliance with the legal framework.

of quality. In addition, the amended Higher Education Act makes a strong point of higher education institutions' responsibilities for implementing internal quality control systems and designates their effective and efficient operation as an aspect of external monitoring and evaluation, carried out by the National Evaluation and Accreditation Agency. The change of the paradigm is illustrated by comparing the legal provisions for institutional and programme accreditation set by the Higher Education Act before and after the amendments.

Institutional accreditation legal definitions:

2004 Higher Education Act	1999 Higher Education Act
An outcome of the evaluation of how effective and efficient is the higher education institution in maintaining, monitoring and improving the quality of education in the fields of education on offer.	Determines conformity of internal arrangements and all activities of the higher education institution and its units with the higher education act and the state requirements.

Programme accreditation legal definitions:

2004 Higher Education Act	1999 Higher Education Act
An outcome of evaluation, based on examination of the quality of student learning in all types and forms of study and in particular qualification levels.	An evaluation of the quality of education in individual courses and programmes of study.

Thus the focus of institutional accreditation shifted from conformity with the law to internal quality assurance and quality enhancement arrangements set by the institution. In programme accreditation, the evaluation of student learning experience is in focus now, rather than compliance with the uniform state requirements, designed in a prescriptive form of national curricula. In consistence with this new approach, the higher education institutions' responsibilities are clearly identified with the quality of provision and research, which they are legally obliged to assure through a formal quality management system. The system has to be included into the statute of the higher education institution and there must be a place in it for a regular feedback from students (HEA, 1995; article6(4); 6(5)).

Following the legal change, the present quality method emphasises outputs rather than inputs to quality. What matters now is whether institutions achieve predetermined levels of quality in the design, delivery and evaluation of higher education courses and awards. In the guidelines to accreditation the Accreditation Council defines institutional and programme accreditation as both based on analysis of the quality of education, research and the management of the institution (NEAA, 2005, p. 91). This indicates a significant change of perception about quality and quality assurance of higher education in Bulgaria.

Whether this conceptual shift could bring about system transformations is a valid question, since numerous legal changes in the last decade proved to be unable to help improving the quality of higher education. It would be worthwhile, therefore, to consider the prospects for improved quality in the sector under the present situation. In addition, the influence of the present framework of quality assurance system over its orientation to improvement or accountability needs to be considered.

2.2. The government and public legitimacy of the new accreditation model

The new legal setting provides a clear line between the role and responsibilities of the major legislative and governing bodies that make the final decision about the establishment of a higher education institution, or a faculty, or a branch, and the accreditation agency role in providing the government and the wider public with independently produced conclusions and recommendations as an outcome of its accreditation processes and procedures. Thus the independent role of the agency as professional body with a mission in external quality assurance is strengthened.

The legal change added to the powers of the National Assembly as a licensing body with regard to opening and closing down of faculties providing courses and degrees in the field of regulated professions. This is attached to the already existing powers for deciding about establishment, transformation and closing down of higher education institutions. All such decisions require assurance from the National Evaluation and Accreditation Agency, based on an *ex ante* evaluation. The new legal setting preserves the Council of Ministers' decision-making powers regarding the establishment and closing down of faculties, institutes, branch campuses and colleges inside state universities. The amendments strengthened the role of the Minister of Education and Science in controlling whether the higher education institutions respect the law. In cases of legal infringement he/she can address the National Evaluation and Accreditation Agency with a proposal to revoke the accreditation status by initiating a re-accreditation. The licensing and approval powers of the above-mentioned bodies are all based on the external quality assurance methods developed and used by the National Evaluation and Accreditation Agency as an organisation established to maintain the responsibility of the state to provide transparent measures for quality assurance (Nyborg, p. 356).

The National Evaluation and Accreditation Agency (NEAA) is a governmental body with a key co-ordinating role in accreditation in Bulgaria. As a public establishment recognised by law (that is, the Higher Education Act), its accreditation decisions and its conclusions about the quality of the projects for the establishment of new institutions, faculties and branches have formal consequences for higher education institutions and their activities. Only accredited institutions can run their teaching and research activities and their academic awards are recognised only upon subject- or programme-level accreditation. Only accredited institutions and subjects are liable for public funding and the volume of funding depends on the accreditation grade rate of a particular institution and subject.

The public legitimacy of the agency is prompted by a legal obligation to make publicly available its accreditation decisions and the provisions for an appeals procedure against these decisions. An additional source for public credibility of the agency conclusions and recommendations lies in its independent status and professional management. With its intermediary position between the state and the universities, the agency represents public interests in the assurance of good quality of education for all students. A growing understanding of the need for professional management of the processes and criteria developed and used by the agency is marked by the new position of the Accreditation Council members and the Standing Committees' chairpersons. They are appointed on a full-time basis in the agency for their six- or three-year terms of office respectively, so that they can be independent of their universities and devote relevant amounts of time to running the agency business.

The Accreditation Council and its chairperson, who is also the agency president, is the agency governing body. The Council is appointed by the prime minister, on a quota principle, which represents the interests of universities (six seats, nominated by the Rectors' Conference), scientific organisations (two seats, nominated by the Bulgarian Academy of Sciences and the National Centre for Agricultural Science) and the government (two nominees of the minister of education and science and one of the prime minister, who is usually the agency president). The number of seats in the Accreditation Council is determined in the Higher Education Act and it currently consists of 11 members (compared to nine until 2004). The interests of the Rectors' Conference represent the majority of the Council (six members). There is a new position in it, that of vice-president, who is responsible for the post-accreditation monitoring. The vice-president is appointed by the prime minister from the Rectors' Conference quota.

The Act also transfers accreditation decision-making powers to the eight subject-based Standing Committees of the Agency with regard to the subject-level accreditation.

Currently all members of the Council and of the Standing Committees are senior academics coming from various subject fields and types of institutions and some have background experience in higher education management and governance. Nonetheless, both groups are occasionally challenged in reaching consistency in their conclusions and decisions in view of the great variety and considerable amount of procedures set by the legal framework.

The main forms of accreditation are first at the level of a university as a whole, and second at the level of the individual subject. The agency also evaluates projects for the establishment of new institutions, new faculties and branches, and new subjects. Evaluation and accreditation of programmes, leading to qualifications in the so-called "regulated professions" is under specific regulations and the agency organises for these separate procedures. Accreditation of doctoral programmes is also carried separately from the subject accreditation. In effect, the number of external evaluations expanded to 10 different types. All these are supplemented by procedures for post-accreditation monitoring and control – a new function for the agency, brought with the legal change in 2004. The established new unit is responsible for the organisation and implementation of the follow-up processes. It became operational in October 2005.

Thus almost each and every activity of the university falls in the scope of accreditation, which leads to unnecessary duplication and the phenomenon of "accreditation fatigue" in the academic community.

Maybe a small compensation for the universities is that now the length of the cycle depends on the accreditation result and varies from six years to eighteen months for institutions and subjects that failed to get accredited. As a result, the institutions and programmes performing well enjoy a longer period (a maximum of six years) of their accreditation validity.

3. Outcomes and lessons learned

The revised quality assurance model became operational in 2005 and since then 70% of all higher education institutions have been accredited or re-accredited.

The accreditation results so far demonstrate that universities have made significant progress in developing and implementing their internal quality assurance system on a more systematic basis. The majority of institutions have officially introduced their systems. Among the first outcomes are improved student achievement rates and improved research productivity of academic staff. These are related to the massive internal reviews of existing programmes and the following update in many and close-down of some programmes. Other typical measures taken by universities include greater financial autonomy for faculty research and a strong connection between staff promotion and research productivity.

In September 2005 the Accreditation Council approved protocols for student participation in institutional evaluations, thus ensuring the student voice in external quality reviews. The model programme for site visits of agency peer experts includes interviews with employers of the university graduates. For smaller higher education institutions, providing financial resources for effective and efficient work of already-introduced quality assurance systems is a real problem. Many others raise concerns whether they will be able to support financially their newly implemented quality systems over a longer period.

The first session of subject accreditation started in January 2006 and already 20 subject fields (out of 52) are under review. According to the national schedule adopted by the agency in September 2005, all 52 subject fields will be reviewed by July 2009. The method shifts the focus of institutional and programme reviews to the processes and structures set by the institution in order to ensure the quality and standards of its academic programmes, rather than compliance with the law. The subject-level approach in programme accreditation is expected to allow for a broader, cross-sector analysis of a particular subject field and to help identify issues that need to be addressed nationally. It also allows the reviewers to concentrate on the characteristic features of qualification degrees as a main unit of assessment, which might contribute to the future establishment of national reference points regarding the standards of qualifications.

The accreditation prerogatives of the agency prompt high expectations on the part of the government, and the Ministry of Education and Science in particular, as to its ability to reform the sector and improve the quality of higher education. While quality and its assurance at all times are the prime responsibility of the higher education institutions, the external quality assurance processes used by the agency can strengthen institutions and reinforce their efforts to improve quality. This requires that the agency develop further as a competent and trustworthy partner of the institutions, in which conclusions and decisions are reached in a consistent manner and in accordance with declared principles (ENQA, 2005).

Two principal concerns arise from the discussion on agency responsibilities regarding quality assurance. First, strong governmental influence over the agency may easily become an obstacle to its transition from an authority exercising control over higher education institutions to one capable of advising and acting as a professional partner in line with the vision of the role of external monitoring and evaluation in helping institutions to improve the quality of higher education and research. Thus the opportunity to set the new quality assurance framework on an improvement-oriented path seems endangered. With the expanding scope of accreditation (the number of types of evaluation has increased from six to ten since 2004) there is a danger of too much preoccupation of higher education institutions with accountability activities. The quality assurance framework orientation towards accountability is therefore quite clear. This is in contrast with the official policy statements of the last two governments and their strategic documents in the sector, describing quality improvement in Bulgarian higher education as a top priority (Government strategy 2003-2006).

The place of students and employers under the new framework is another source of concern. Institutions rarely provide opportunities for students to become involved in internal quality assurance processes. Although a widespread practice in our universities, student feedback questionnaires and the information contained in these are not systematically used as grounds for correcting or improving existing practices. While the place of student feedback in internal quality assurance processes is a legal requirement, there is no legal provision for employers. They are typically excluded from the internal processes of programme design and approval. Thus the decisions for course and programme content are not supported by valuable and up-to-date information about the skill needs of the job market in a particular field, where graduates are expected to apply their qualifications. Employers are not involved in the accreditation decision-making process either, but external evaluators meet them upon their site visit and take into consideration their opinion in their evaluation reports.

Although no subject field has yet to be evaluated and accredited according to the new model, feedback reports from the first review team reveal issues for consideration in several areas:

- the process of preparation of the self-evaluation reports apparently caused problems to some universities and colleges that lack sufficient internal integrity and have problems with communication between units and programmes;
- the implementation of the credit accumulation and transfer system is lagging behind the schedule in many universities and programmes, especially when these enjoy high student interest and a good reputation;
- students' and employers' interests are rarely taken into account in programme design, monitoring and approval;
- internal arrangements for doctoral studies prevent students from timely transition to the final stage of their defence, particularly in the social sciences and humanities;
- ageing staff is becoming a common problem.

Discussions with university managers and student representatives point to the lack of enthusiasm for reforms and criticism about the "top-down" approach and hasty action of the government and the legislators in introducing change.

A prerequisite for successful implementation of the revised quality assurance framework in Bulgaria is the engagement of universities with quality and quality improvement. In this process the development of a sense of ownership of the quality processes at all levels of the individual institution is of vital importance. For this to take place, institutional autonomy is essential. The outline of trends in quality assurance practices points to the relationship between the level of autonomy and the successful implementation of quality assurance processes and procedures in universities across Europe (Trends IV Report, 2005). The autonomy of Bulgarian universities is legally guaranteed by the Higher Education Act, yet there is some controversy between the legal definition of autonomy and the texts defining the scope and content of autonomy. What the notion of autonomy comprises according to the law is "freedom in determining educational programmes and content, rules of study, standards and criteria for student enrolment and graduation, as well as their research agendas". What is missing is determination of internal organisation, selection and promotion of the teaching staff. Universities' internal organisation is mirrored in their statutes and these in turn are comprehensively prescribed by the law. Staff selection and promotion is subject to external regulation by a separate law and a governmental body, namely the Academic Titles and Awards Committee. In this situation internal institutional management would have a limited role and managers would have scattered responsibilities. This results in a lack of internal integrity, which is an important condition for successful organisational reform. At this point we come to the issue of quality assurance, which at the level of the institution as a whole is at its best a set of unrelated instruments.

4. The way forward

4.1. Internal quality assurance processes need to be sufficiently financed on a continuous basis, if we want to see good results.

4.2. Currently, employers' interests are presented in reviewers' meetings at their site visits in the institution. But higher education institutions should organise meetings with employers on a regular basis and should inform their decisions about course and programme design and approval with employers' views. The massive initiative of Bulgarian universities in setting up career guidance centres in the last couple of years provides a forum for regular contacts between the graduates and their employers. This positive step of establishing institutional contacts with employers needs to reach further to the university programme managers and designers.

4.3. Students are already involved in external quality assurance and with their growing awareness and experience in the quality issues they can contribute significantly to the quality enhancement of their own institutions and programmes. The quality management bodies inside the higher education institutions should involve students on a more systematic basis than they are doing at present.

4.4. The involvement of international reviewers from reputable universities and agencies must be financially supported by the government, as well as co-operation between the quality assurance agencies.

4.5. The implementation of the Bergen standards implies a level of autonomy for the national agency not just in terms of its operational independence from other bodies, but from the Higher Education Act, which is prescriptive and detailed in issues dealing with daily routines of the agency. The national agency freedom to independently define its methods and criteria for external evaluation needs to be legally regulated. Such regulation should be limited to a small set of requirements to the agency like: (a) following predetermined goals and objectives of the external quality assurance processes and procedures; (b) not implementing external quality assurance processes and procedures before consulting with other stakeholders, including higher education institutions; (c) publishing these with detailed descriptions of criteria and procedures for evaluation, accreditation and follow-up.

4.6. Quality can and should be improved by the higher education institutions, not by the ministry or agency. Institutions need to have more power over their internal affairs in order to fulfil their responsibility for quality. Good practice in quality assurance across European universities shows that good quality is associated with greater institutional autonomy (Trends IV Report, 2005). With their growing confidence in assuring quality, Bulgarian universities may gradually take over periodic review of their courses and programmes and the agency would then only check from time to time the effectiveness of their internal quality assurance arrangements. Such an approach has been recently under discussion among academic circles and it leaves room for reconsideration of the future role of the national agency as a partner and consultant to universities in their efforts to enhance the quality.

4.7. Last but not least, future considerations of the quality assurance concept in Bulgaria should take into account that whenever evaluation of quality is taken to form the basis for accreditation decisions, it is most likely that accountability processes rather than improvement or enhancement processes will occur.

References

"Realising the European Higher Education Area", Communiqué of the Conference of Ministers responsible for Higher Education, Berlin, 19 September 2003.

"The European Higher Education Area – Achieving the Goals", Communiqué of the Conference of Ministers responsible for Higher Education, Bergen, 19-20 May 2005.

ENQA (2005), "Standards and guidelines for quality assurance in the European Higher Education Area", adopted by the Bergen Conference of European Ministers responsible for Higher Education, May 2005.

Glasgow Declaration (2005), *Strong Universities for a Strong Europe,* EUA.

Higher Education Act (2004), www.apisnet.net/en

Management Plan of the Government of the Republic of Bulgaria 2001-2005 (2000), www.mdaar.government.bg

National Evaluation and Accreditation Agency (2005), *Evaluation and Accreditation of Higher Education Institutions.* ABAGAR Publishing House, Veliko Tarnovo.

Nyborg, Per, *Higher Education in Europe.* Vol. XXVIII, No.3, 2003.

Reichert, Sybille and Tauch, Christian (2005), Trends IV Report: *European Universities Implementing Bologna.* EUA.

The Irish approach

Fergal Costello

The aim of this paper is to outline the current position of quality assurance systems in Irish higher education, to explain the development of those systems, and to look to possible directions for development into the future. The views expressed are personal, reflecting my own experience of nearly five years' work in the Higher Education Authority, the funding and policy agency for Irish higher education.[11] It should be noted that until this year the remit of the HEA extended only to the university sector, and there has been proportionately less involvement with the procedures in place in the institutes of technology and the Dublin Institute of Technology (DIT); this is reflected in this paper.

1. Introduction

"This systematic organisation and promotion of quality assurance at the universities themselves is … unparalleled in any other country in Europe, or indeed in the United States and Canada. The system would appear to strike the right tone and combination of public interest, accountability, and university autonomy. It encourages a greater focus on quality and improvement than some systems worldwide, while at the same time being less intrusive than some other systems in Europe."[12]

In Ireland a high standard of third-level education is credited as being an important factor in the strong growth of the Irish economy from the 1990s onwards. With ever-increasing international competition and the move towards the creation of a knowledge economy the quality of Irish third-level education is a vital public policy issue. In addition the Bologna Process with its aim of creating a European Higher Education Area by 2010 also stresses the importance of quality assurance.

Ireland has a binary system of higher education. One part is formed by the universities and colleges of education and the other part is made up of the institutes of technology and Dublin Institute of Technology. The institutes of technology are regionally based and have a vocational role, and are more focused on technical courses.

2. The basis for quality assurance

2.1. Universities

The Universities Act 1997 established the quality assurance process currently in place. However, prior to the Act there were more informal elements of quality

---

11. The HEA (set up following the HEA Act 1971) is the statutory planning and development body for higher education and research in Ireland. It has wide advisory powers throughout third-level education and is the funding authority for the universities and some designated higher education institutions.

12. European University Association (EUA) (2005), p. 12.

review in place, such as "involvement of external examiners in primary and higher degrees, peer-review system of research publication, peer-review system of assessing applications for research grants, ... involvement of staff as peer reviewers and external examiners internationally, feedback related to the employability of graduates and their progression to prestigious international graduate programmes and external membership of selection groups for academic appointments."[13]

2.1.1. The 1997 legislation

Section 35 of the Universities Act 1997 requires the governing authority:

> "to establish procedures for quality assurance aimed at improving the quality of education and related services provided by the university.
>
> These procedures shall include –
>> (a) the evaluation, at regular intervals and in any case not less than once in every 10 years or such longer period as may be determined by the university in agreement with An tUdarás, of each department and, where appropriate, faculty of the university in the first instance and by persons other than employees, who are competent to make national and international comparisons on the quality of teaching and research and the provision of other services at university level, and
>>
>> (b) assessment by those, including students availing of the teaching, research and other services provided by the university."[14]

2.1.2. Main points of interest

- The Universities Act was the first piece of legislation to set out specifically the responsibilities of the universities for quality improvement and quality assurance.
- The scope of the legislation is wide; the quality review applies not only to teaching and learning, but also to research, administration and all other activity in the universities.
- The autonomy of the universities is preserved as the Act sets out that it is the responsibility of the governing authority of each university to initiate the quality review.
- The quality assurance evaluation has to take place at least every ten years, initially including the employees of the university, then by persons other than employees who are competent to make national and international comparisons on the quality of teaching and research and the provision of other services at university level.

---

13. Conference of Heads of Irish Universities (CHIU) (2003), p. 18.
14. Universities Act 1997, Section 35.1.

- There must also be assessment by those using the teaching, research and other services provided by the university, including students.
- Findings must be published and implemented where possible.
- At least every fifteen years, in consultation with the HEA, the governing authority must arrange for a review of the effectiveness of the quality assurance procedures. This review must be published and presented to the Minister for Education and Science.
- Under Section 49, the HEA may also review the procedures established. Section 49 also gives the HEA statutory responsibility to assist the universities in achieving the objectives set out in the Act in relation to quality assurance.[15]

2.2. Quality assurance in the institutes of technology

The provisions for quality assurance in the 13 institutes of technology and DIT are set out in separate legislation, the Qualifications Act of 2000. This Act established the Higher Education and Training Awards Council with responsibility to make awards for non-university higher education courses. The Act also provided for a process whereby the council could delegate to the individual institutes the right to make their own awards, and to manage their own quality assurance processes. Considerable work has been applied in this area since the Act, and all institutes now have at least some level of delegated authority.

DIT operates within a separate framework. DIT has since 1992 had the power to make its own awards. Since the Act of 2000, DIT also has the authority to manage its own quality assurance procedures, subject to review by the National Qualifications Authority.

3. The practice of quality assurance in the Irish third-level sector

3.1. Quality assurance in Irish universities

To enable a common approach to quality assurance across the university sector a large number of actors are involved in university quality assurance.

3.1.1. The Irish Universities Quality Board (IUQB)

The IUQB was established in 2002. The universities established the IUQB to aid inter-university co-operation in quality assurance. The IUQB approves the agencies that conduct the periodic reviews of quality assurance procedures in the Irish universities and provides reports on this process to the Council of the Irish Universities Association (IUA) and to the Higher Education Authority. The IUQB also receives the annual report of the executive committee on the implementation of these procedures and

---

15. CHIU (2003), p. 18, Universities Act 1997.

reports on any issues arising to the IUA and the HEA. The IUQB also is mandated to organise projects aimed at improving the quality of teaching and learning, research and strategic planning in the universities.[16]

3.1.2. The Quality Promotion Committee

Each university has a quality promotion committee. Usually this committee is a sub-committee of the Governing Authority or Academic Council. A quality promotion unit generally co-ordinates the daily work and is often headed by a senior academic with one or two assistants and reports directly to either the Registrar or the President.[17]

3.1.3. The Irish Universities Association (formerly the Conference of Heads of Irish Universities)

The IUA is the representative body of the heads of the seven Irish universities.

3.1.4. The European University Association (EUA)

The EUA is the representative organisation of European universities. The EUA's mission is to promote the development of a coherent system of European higher education and research.[18]

3.1.5. Students, staff and other stakeholders

Universities have a wide range of internal (staff, students) and external stakeholders (includes graduates, employers and professional bodies, taxpayers, the local and national community, social partners, government and public authorities, the EU and relevant international agencies). All these stakeholders are legitimately interested in the performance of the institutions and hence in the quality of the service provided by the institutions. The universities need to assess and take account of the opinions of this wide range of stakeholders.[19]

Students often participate in the quality review by way of questionnaires and focus groups. Indeed, the legislation explicitly states that students need to be consulted during the quality review. All the staff members of a unit are invited to contribute to the work involved in the self-assessment report and indeed are expected to contribute to it. Also, the results of anonymous staff questionnaires are included in the self-assessment report. Staff also are entitled to private access to the peer review group. Employers and graduates are also often invited to meet privately with the peer review group.[20]

---

16. www.iuqb.ie.
17. EUA (2005), p. 11.
18. www.eua.be/eua/en/about_eua.jspx.
19. CHIU (2003), p. 29.
20. IUQB, p. 3.

3.2. How is the quality assessment carried out?[21]

3.2.1. The self-assessment

The first step is the self-assessment. This involves the unit answering four basic questions:

(1) What are you trying to do?

(Mission, aims, objectives and their appropriateness, how the university positions itself locally, nationally, internationally.)

(2) How are you trying to do it?

(Processes, procedures, practices in place and analysis of their effectiveness.)

(3) How do you know it works?

(Feedback systems in place, in particular quality monitoring and quality management.)

(4) How do you change in order to improve?
(Strategic planning, capacity and willingness to change.)[22]

In order for the unit to answer these questions, it has to evaluate the performance of its functions, services and administration. The self-assessment report provides the peer review group with essential information to prepare both the review visit and the final review report. The preparation of self-assessment reports follows essentially the same process for all units within an institution. However, the content of reports will vary with the outline of the unit, for example, the report from an academic department will differ from that of an administrative unit.

3.2.2. The peer review group

After the completion of the self-assessment report the unit is visited by a peer review group, which includes at least two external experts. The length of the visit of the peer review group is usually two to three days, but this may vary depending on the complexity of the work of the unit. The quality office organises the structure and timetable of the visit in advance in consultation with the unit being reviewed. The peer review group report is also concerned with the four questions outlined above, but with special emphasis on the fourth question – How do you change in order to improve? The review group usually identifies the strengths and weaknesses of the unit, points to examples of good practice to be disseminated throughout the university, and makes constructive recommendations on matters that require improvement, based on consideration of the self-assessment documentation and the outcomes of the site visit.

---

21. The main source for this section is CHIU (2003), pp. 42-50.
22. EUA (2005), pp. 8, 9.

When the draft report of the review group is completed, the unit's co-ordinating committee is invited to indicate any errors of fact. The final report is then distributed to the relevant areas of the university, for example the governing authority, all members of staff of the unit and others concerned.

3.2.3. Publication and implementation

Section 35 of the Universities Act provides for the publication of findings arising out of the quality review process, and also compels the governing authority to implement the findings, having regard to the available resources and unless it would be unreasonable to do so. There are common mechanisms across the seven universities to ensure that the recommendations made in the peer review group report are properly adhered to in accordance with the Universities Act and that maximum benefit is gained from the quality review. Usually after the review, a quality improvement plan is drawn up by the relevant unit in consultation with the university with the aim of implementing the recommendation of the review group. This plan is then to be implemented by the unit with the support of the university. This may entail requests for additional funds from the relevant university authorities.

3.2.4. Response

The peer review group reports and the quality improvement plans are examined by the relevant university decision-making bodies, such as the faculty or university management group. These bodies then issue a formal written response which concentrates on areas that have resource implications for the faculty or university.[23]

One of the important outcomes from the formal establishment of a quality review process is that the concept of quality is becoming built into discussions at many levels across each university campus. Such discussions, combined with the quality assessment and evaluation procedures, are leading to higher levels of quality awareness and a burgeoning quality culture across the universities. An important strength of the Irish system of quality assurance is that academics with a lot of experience of how universities operate are leading the process.[24]

3.3. Quality assurance in the institutes of technology

HETAC has developed procedures for external quality assurance of the institutes of technology. A major element of these procedures is programme validation. This involves a panel of experts advising HETAC on whether the individual institutions and programmes meet the set criteria. In their self-evaluation report HETAC points out that using programme validation as a main mechanism for quality assurance standards

---

23. CHIU (2003), pp. 42-50.
24. EUA (2005), p. 11.

as envisaged in the Qualifications (Education and Training) Act 1999 reflected international practice in the mid-1990s. However, HETAC also notes that current international practice reflects increased emphasis on institutional quality assurance.

The delegation of authority to make awards to the institutes of technology and DIT has enabled HETAC to change focus onto institutional quality assurance. The Qualifications (Education and Training) Act 1999 did provide for recognised institutions to make awards and validate programmes themselves. The procedure for attaining this power involves institutes drawing up a self-evaluation report that sufficiently meets the set criteria of HETAC and NQAI. After the report there is a panel visit and a report to HETAC on whether or not the criteria have been met. After this HETAC makes its decision, which is subject to agreement by the NQAI.

HETAC has established two committees with the responsibility for accrediting programmes. These are the Programme Accreditation Committee (PAC) and the Research Degree Programme Committee (RDPC). They have delegated validation powers and hence can make decisions on individual applications for accreditation and also advise on policy development. The delegation of authority for research awards is linked by HETAC to its policy on accreditation to maintain research registers. For taught programmes, delegation is made by award-type in the national framework. However, delegation is by discipline for research degree programmes. According to HETAC's self-evaluation report this approach has ensured that confidence is maintained in the standards. The review process is rigorous and has a strong international input, the resulting reports are published and there is a high level of engagement with the process within the sector. Hence the approach is currently considered to be effective.[25]

3.3.1. Agreement on quality assurance procedures

Under the Qualifications (Education and Training) Act 1999 providers of higher education and training programmes that are validated by HETAC, or to whom HETAC has delegated powers to make awards, need to agree their quality assurance procedures with HETAC. The HETAC self-evaluation report notes that the process involved in agreeing the quality assurance procedures has encouraged the providers of the courses to take ownership of their own quality assurance functions. Therefore, a culture shift is taking place away from compliance with external requirements and towards institutions taking the responsibility for maintaining standards and enhancing the learner experience.

All institutions are to be reviewed at periodic intervals. A review of the quality assurance procedures is to take place within five years of the initial agreement of quality assurance procedures between the institutes and HETAC. In addition, a review of delegation of authority has to take place at least once every five years. In order to avoid over-review of institutions, HETAC combines these two reviews.[26]

---

25. HETAC (2006), pp. 11-20.
26. HETAC (2006), pp. 11-20.

3.4. Quality assurance in DIT

DIT received degree-awarding powers in 1997. DIT also undertook responsibility for its own quality assurance. Under the Qualifications (Education and Training) Act 1999 DIT is obliged to agree its quality assurance procedures with the NQAI. The NQAI can make recommendations to DIT regarding these and the NQAI and DIT have to ensure that the procedures in place are subject to periodic external review. These policies and procedures emphasise quality enhancement and the development of institution-wide quality processes. The procedures involve "preliminary course approval, the formal validation of new courses, examination and assessment procedures, including the use of external examiners for each course every year (except the apprenticeship programmes), and the regular monitoring of existing courses".[27]

The quality assurance system in DIT focuses on school-based reviews and hence one review covers a range of courses and support/administrative procedures. This enables a broad picture to be taken of how courses interact and are supported. There are also plans for a faculty review which would incorporate teaching and learning, research, service and administration.

There is also regular monitoring of existing courses, via student feedback provided to the lecturer through a standard DIT-wide form. Courses are also monitored through a five-yearly academic review which examines each programme in detail to establish if the course should continue as it is, continue in a modified form or cease to operate.

The DIT Academic Council has primary responsibility for quality assurance, and to this end has established an academic quality assurance committee as a standing sub-committee. The system in DIT is seen to be evolving and flexible and capable of responding to strategic needs as they arise.[28]

4. Reviews of the Irish quality assurance systems

4.1. The EUA review of quality assurance in Irish universities

Under the 1997 Universities Act the procedures in place for the university quality assurance process must be reviewed at least every ten years. To this end the IUQB and the HEA jointly commissioned this review by the EUA in 2003. According to the EUA "the review is designed to ensure that the university system and its stakeholders gain maximum benefit from comprehensive reviews by teams of experienced international quality assurance experts, and that the procedures and processes in place in Irish universities can be reviewed against best practice internationally".[29]

---

27. EUA (2005), p. 7.
28. EUA (2006), pp. 7-11.
29. EUA (2005), p. 3.

4.2. Findings of the EUA review

4.2.1. Strengths of the quality assurance process

In its report, the EUA confirmed that Ireland's universities have met and surpassed their statutory obligations and have developed strong quality cultures and systems. The EUA review states that the EUA team was impressed by "the well organised systems in place, by the seriousness of the approach in each university to the quality assurance process, and by the amount of work undertaken by departments, faculties, service units and the university leadership and administration to ensure the success of these procedures".[30]

The EUA review found that the self-assessment process at unit level is a vital element in the overall quality assurance process as it increases the ownership of whatever quality improvement measures are found to be necessary. The EUA suggests that the unit under review can actually learn more through an honest and thorough self-assessment than through the subsequent peer review. The EUA team also noted that the self-assessment processes at unit level in each university appeared to be conducted in a positive way.

4.2.2. EUA recommendations

For the second round of university self-assessments, the EUA recommends that the choice of peer review team members be wider and more flexible. It suggests that it may be useful to have more international members as this would be an opportunity to benchmark Irish universities against a wider variety of universities and higher education systems. The EUA review also recommended that the unit under review should have a minimal input as to who composes the peer review group. It suggests that this could be done by having the unit propose an external expert who could then put forward a shortlist of potential peers. The EUA also advises that the terms of reference and the guidelines for peer reviewers be updated. The reviewers should have a broader definition of quality, to include internationalisation, interdisciplinarity and research and to support strategic change. The EUA also recommends a clear distinction between the "recommendations which can be implemented without significant additional resources and those which do indeed require new investment".[31] The peer review reports should be clear and unambiguous to ensure that responsibility for the implementation of their recommendations is assigned to the appropriate level.

The EUA review queried the length of time the peer review takes. As the plan has to be discussed and negotiated at various steps in each university's structure, it can often take almost a year. As the self-assessment can also take up to a year, this means that the process can take two years. The EUA considers this to be considerably too long as the context will have changed before the outcomes have been agreed. The

---

30. EUA (2005), p. 11.
31. EUA (2005), p. 18.

EUA also points out that it is vital that the quality assurance process receives the necessary support from senior management and governance in the universities and that university governing authorities and executives follow up on the quality improvement plan and support its implementation as, if they do not, this could demotivate the staff. The HEA has put money in place to support quality improvement initiatives. Also, most universities have put small funds in place to support the quality improvement initiatives. The EUA team cautioned against viewing quality assurance only in the context of these dedicated funds, and recommended that universities view their entire budget as quality improvement funds, instead of just small segments of it.

A weakness of the quality review focusing on the individual departments is that it tends to reinforce the existing academic structures and boundaries by not questioning the need for those boundaries. The majority of Irish universities have a large number of departments and units, which can often be small, and they are usually based on discipline. The format of higher education is changing from a large number of small departments to a smaller number of larger departments. This is necessary to strengthen inter-disciplinary processes and to increase collective responsibility. Reviews focusing on single departments mean that interdisciplinary issues or programmes are not systematically addressed as they may fall between academic departments. In a small number of cases where similar departments or units were grouped together for the quality review this was found to be a very useful process. The EUA recommends that the guidelines for self-assessment and peer reviews explicitly recommend that all relevant interdisciplinary work be within the scope of the quality review.

There is a non-aggressive approach to unit/department participation in the quality review. Units have tended to nominate themselves for review and also peer pressure is encouraging units to seek review. This approach has advantages as it means that the review can build on goodwill and the readiness of the units to participate. However, the main weakness in this approach is that it means that the schedule for quality review of the various departments or units is not based on any strategic plans at the university or linked to major opportunities/challenges or other strategic cycles such as an executive succession in a particular faculty or school, professional accreditation processes under way that involve certain departments, or strategic planning. The EUA team recommends that in the next quality review phase the timings be approached in a more strategic manner. The EUA suggested that having a review cycle of ten or even seven years is too long, as by the time the next review of a department is due, the findings of the last review will be out of date and hence the next review will not be able to build on the findings of the previous one. Additionally, the universities need to decide whether the second round of evaluations needs to cover all units again or whether it should concentrate on the weaknesses found during the first quality review and issues, such as interdisciplinary work, that were not necessarily covered in the first cycle.

The EUA also highlighted the potential risk that in the medium term the dedicated quality promotion units in each university could assume the responsibility for quality assurance away from the basic department or service unit. The EUA does stress that the promotion units have "been doing excellent work". However, they could become increasingly relied on and therefore focus must be kept on the useful outcomes of the quality assurance process and not just on the process of the quality assurance review.

As mentioned above, there were elements of a quality assurance system in place long before the 1997 Universities Act. However, the EUA team noted that there are few if any formal links between these aspects of quality assurance and the quality assurance process established as a result of the 1997 legislation. The EUA suggested that establishing or strengthening these links could enable a clearer understanding of how they complement each other as well as resulting in more responsive quality improvement.

Although in theory students have a role in the quality review process, the EUA was surprised to learn how low the level of student participation is in the evaluation of the quality of teaching and learning in Irish universities. Feedback is not obtained from students in all courses and even when it is collected, the EUA found that there is no systematic way to monitor the use of this feedback. The EUA review stresses that student feedback is essential to ensure ongoing improvement of teaching and learning. Therefore Irish universities need to ensure that coherent and regular feedback is obtained for all courses and is fed into the quality review system.[32]

4.3. Review of HETAC

In May 2005, the ministers for education in all the countries partaking in the Bologna Process adopted standards and guidelines for quality assurance in the European Higher Education Area. A requirement of this is that there are periodic external reviews of an external quality assurance agency's activities, to be organised on a national basis.

In this context, and taking into account the requirements for a review of HETAC by the NQAI under the Qualifications Act, NQAI appointed an independent review of HETAC which took place in 2006. The review consisted, first, of a self-evaluation process with a report summarising the result, which was published; subsequently an external review was carried out by an expert panel. This external review included a site visit and resulted in a report, which was also published. HETAC then considered the report and published its plans for implementing recommended changes. As the 2006 review was the first review carried out on HETAC, not all the processes and procedures developed had been implemented yet, such as some relating to the periodic review of institutions. Therefore their effectiveness could not be assessed. The main findings of the review were that HETAC has performed its statutory functions effectively and the review panel was satisfied that the performance also complies with the standards and guidelines for quality assurance in the European Higher Education Area.[33]

---

32. EUA (2005), pp. 7-19.
33. HETAC (2006), pp. 4, 11, 16.

4.4. The DIT quality review process

DIT is required to undergo an external review of its quality procedures every three to seven years. The first review of DIT's procedures was commissioned jointly by DIT and NQAI in 2004. The aim of the review was to assess DIT's ability to change by examining its strategic planning and internal quality culture.

The review by the EUA was similar to the quality assurance review performed by the universities. It entailed the initial preparation of a self-evaluation report by DIT. This report was guided by the same four questions:

(1) What is the institution trying to do?

(2) How is the institution trying to do it?

(3) How does it know it works?

(4) How can the institution change in order to improve?

The peer review team then went on a site visit to DIT, it requested any extra information or reports that it needed, a second site visit to DIT was carried out, next there was a meeting with the executive of the NQAI to exchange views on the draft findings of the review, the written report was then sent to DIT to be checked for any factual errors, and lastly the finished report was submitted to both DIT and the NQAI.

The follow-up process included the publication of the results of the review by the NQAI as required under Section 39(5) of the Qualifications (Education and Training) Act 1999. After the publication of the results of the review, DIT published the EUA report on its website.[34]

5. Conclusions

The OECD review

In 2003 the OECD Secretariat was invited by the Department of Education and Science to review the Irish higher education system to assess the performance of the sector and recommend how higher education can be enabled to better meet Ireland's strategic objectives for the sector. While this was not specifically a review of quality assurance in Ireland, it did assess the quality of the higher education system in Ireland. Also, like the development of a cohesive quality assurance system in Ireland, it was based on the Irish Government's strategic objective of building on Ireland's strong higher education sector and having Ireland placed in the top OECD ranking in both quality and participation in third-level education. The OECD review group made a total of 52 recommendations, some of which have already been implemented. It recommended that the funding and regulatory functions for the

---

34. National Qualifications Authority of Ireland (NQAI) (2005), pp. 56, 57.

institutes of technology and DIT be unified with the universities under the remit of a single higher education authority in order to better integrate higher education in Ireland. The Institutes of Technology Act 2006 has provided for this change. As this is a new development, it is not yet clear how this will affect the quality assurance practices in third-level institutions in Ireland.[35]

In relation to quality assurance the review supported in principle a common quality assurance framework for both sectors, but noted the need to both:

- let the current system evolve and mature; and
- take account of continuing changes arising out of the Bologna declaration, and to adapt the Irish procedures in line with internationally agreed developments.[36]

The quality assessment procedures in place in Irish higher education institutions are relatively new, with the Universities Act 1997 and the Qualifications (Education and Training) Act 1999 being the relevant legislation. Quality management procedures are complex. Yet it is clear that the quality assurance process is yielding important returns. For example, it is encouraging ownership of the quality process and this bottom-up approach is necessary to legitimise the quality assurance system. Quality assurance procedures are increasingly a part of the daily work at higher-level institutions in Ireland. The second phase of quality assurance reviews should build on the strong foundations currently in place.

The future holds many challenges for the continued development of quality assurance procedures in Ireland. Not least of these is building awareness of quality in Irish third-level education institutions among the Irish general public. Third-level institutions regularly publish details of their quality assurance. However, quality assurance in third-level institutions in Ireland receives a very low level of media coverage and has little impact on the consciousness of the general public. Yet, there is widespread discussion of, and interest in, quality assurance and practice in primary and secondary-level schools in the Irish educational system. There is an ongoing debate on whether league tables of exam results should be made available to the public. Recently, the Department of Education and Science has begun to publish school inspection reports. This move has generated huge media copy and a high level of interest among the general public.

The contrast with the more well-developed, third-level quality assurance, utilising both national and international experts, is instructive. This detailed process receives far less exposure to the general public, and provokes far less interest from the media. On the one hand this may be a sign that the system has bedded down so successfully as to rob it of interest to a media more concerned with crisis. Against this it makes it more difficult to illustrate the scope and depth of change that has taken place in the sector.

---

35. Organisation for Economic Co-operation and Development (OECD) (2004).
36. OECD (2004)

A possible further issue for the future is how to ensure that the quality assurance procedures maintain standards across an institution's courses over the years. Figures from my own agency show that in 2004 the percentage of first class and upper second class honours degrees awarded to undergraduate students has increased in every university since 1998. For example, the number of students at Dublin City University that received a first class honours degree has increased by 10% since 1998. Also, in 2003/2004 56% of all students graduating from Trinity College Dublin (TCD) attained an upper second class honours degree, whereas in 1997/1998 just 14% of all TCD's graduating students achieved an upper second class honours degree. There will always be a level of variation from year to year in courses, due perhaps to different people partaking in the course, leading to different cultures in the class. However, a persistent upwards trend in results could undermine the quality assurance procedures in place. It is vital that quality assurance in third-level institutions ensures that standards remain similar from year to year as otherwise it is likely that the individual degrees from the institutions will be devalued, undermining the reputations of the institutions.

Inconsistencies between universities are also a relevant issue. Attainment of a grade does vary across subject areas and hence the total percentage of students awarded a first class honours degree or an upper second class honours degree will vary from university to university. However, inconsistencies between similar courses in various universities also need to be addressed. According to the 2004 figures, approximately half of all psychology graduates at TCD, NUI Maynooth and NUI Galway attained a first class honours degree, but only 13% did at UCC. This huge distortion in the numbers achieving a first class honours degree in a similar subject area provokes questions. Quality assurance systems should be able to ensure that confidence is maintained in each course at every higher education institution. A possible solution to this is to introduce benchmarking, across courses and previous years, to ensure that the standard of the courses does not decrease or vary considerably from similar courses in other higher education institutions.

Another issue for the future is how to ensure that quality assurance procedures are strong enough to enable very poorly performing departments to improve their performance sufficiently. For example, the 2003 review of medical education in Ireland by the Irish Medical Council had major concerns on the standards of medical education in Ireland. While quality assurance procedures in Irish universities did acknowledge that medical education was in need of reform, they are restricted as to how much quality improvement they could implement, due to budgetary constraints, lack of hospital capacity and so on. The Medical Council Report noted that "Most clinical teachers have major contracts with the health services and minor or non-existent contracts with the universities, which allows the Dean little or no leverage to introduce modern teaching and learning methods... While all schools are committed to quality assurance, in reality there is little professional support and time for this despite the evident benefits to those schools which are involved in QA."[37] The EUA review of NUI Galway found that not only is medical

---

37. Medical Council (2003), www.medicalcouncil.ie/news/publicationsarticle.asp?NID=100&T=N, p. 14.

education in Galway under-funded by comparison to most European countries, it is also under-funded by comparison to some medical faculties in Ireland. There is a need to utilise the quality assurance system more effectively to help address such issues. It should be noted that funding alone may not be the appropriate answer – the link with institutional strategic planning and prioritisation is also essential.

Other issues for the future are the continued development of the national qualifications framework to underpin the quality system. Also, it is vitally important that Irish quality assurance continues to facilitate and support European developments such as the Bologna Declaration of 1999, the Berlin Communiqué 2003, and the Bergen Communiqué 2005.

References

Conference of Heads of Irish Universities (CHIU) (2003), *Framework for Quality in Irish Universities: Meeting the Challenge of Change*, CHIU, Dublin.

European University Association (EUA) (2005), *Review of Quality Assurance in Irish Universities: Sectoral Report*, EUA Institutional Evaluation Programme.

European University Association (EUA) (2006), *Review of Quality Assurance, Dublin Institute of Technology: EUA Reviewer's Report*, EUA

HETAC (2006), *Self-Evaluation Report*, www.hetac.ie

IUQB, 'OECD Submission', www.iuqb.ie

Medical Council (2003), *Review of Medical Schools in Ireland, 2003*, Medical Council, www.medicalcouncil.ie

National Qualifications Authority of Ireland (NQAI) (2005), *Overview of national and international practice concerning the external review of agencies with a substantial role in quality assurance in higher education and review practices concerning public sector agencies in Ireland*, NQAI, Dublin.

Organisation for Economic Co-operation and Development (OECD) (2004), *Review of National Policies for Education: Review of Higher Education in Ireland, Examiner's Report*, France, OECD.

Qualifications (Education and Training) Act 1999

Universities Act 1997, www.eua.be/eua/en/about_eua.jspx
www.iuqb.ie

Quality assurance and the recognition of qualifications

Andrejs Rauhvargers

There is no doubt that a link exists between quality assurance or accreditation on the one side and international recognition of individual qualifications on the other.

The link between quality assurance and recognition is very tight, yet not as trivial as it may seem at first sight. While recognition of qualifications is impossible without knowing about the quality of the particular programme and the institution behind the qualification, it cannot be granted based on quality indicators alone (1).

Since 2001 regular meetings between representatives of the European Quality Assurance Association (ENQA) and European recognition networks ENIC and NARIC have served as a platform for the exchange of views and have no doubt led to a better understanding between quality assurance and recognition specialists.

1. Some features of recognition

To assess a qualification fairly means to adequately position it in the grid of qualifications of the receiving country. The outcome of assessment is therefore dependent not only on the features of the higher education system from which the qualification originates, but also on those of the host system and the differences between the two higher education systems.

The best practice in recognition of foreign qualifications, as codified in the Lisbon Recognition Convention for academic recognition and the Directives establishing the general system for professional recognition, has moved from seeking "equivalence" towards recognition if the differences between the foreign qualification and the host country's prototype are not substantial (2) (article VI.1). Furthermore, because qualifications of comparable levels may show considerable differences in terms of function, profile and learning outcomes, these differences should be considered in view of the purpose for which recognition is sought – for example, further studies in a particular programme or employment in a non-regulated profession; cf. (3).

While the 2005 stocktaking exercise (4) demonstrated the progress in ratification of the Lisbon Recognition Convention, there are still problems related to its practical implementation. The official Bologna seminar on recognition in Riga on 3-4 December 2004 indicated that unfortunately some countries having signed and ratified the Lisbon Recognition Convention have not properly transposed the principles of the Convention in their national legislation (5). As a result, in these countries, recognition practices may still include seeking full equivalence (or even applying nostrification procedure) of foreign qualifications.

In their Bergen communiqué, ministers (6) agreed to draw up national plans for improving the recognition system of foreign qualifications. Hopefully the implementation of the Lisbon Recognition Convention will be included in the 2007 stocktaking exercise.

1.1. Benefits brought to recognition by quality assurance

Quality assurance is a very important first step in individual recognition.

A credential evaluator needs to know that the qualification has been earned at an institution or in a programme of sufficient quality. Once that has been established, however, the more individualised work begins – the credential evaluator can then assess the other components of the qualification: workload, level, profile, learning outcomes, whilst considering the aim for which recognition of qualification is sought.

In 1997, when the Lisbon Recognition Convention was adopted, nationally organised quality assurance systems were just emerging. Therefore the issue of the quality of qualifications had to be left to trust between countries party to the convention, which were obliged to compile and publish lists of state-recognised institutions; cf. article VIII.2 of the Lisbon Recognition Convention (2).

At present credential evaluators can expect much more from their quality assurance counterparts. First, at this stage when national quality assurance systems have been created in practically all countries involved in the Bologna process, it is difficult to imagine that countries would compile lists of their state-recognised institutions and programmes without referring to the results of national quality assurance of the institutions or their programmes in question.

To justify what has been said above, the overarching qualifications framework for the European Higher Education Area (EHEA) in addition to workload, level, profile and learning outcomes also includes quality assurance as one of the components of a qualification. Moreover, when creating the national qualifications frameworks, countries should include qualifications in their national framework using a transparent procedure, which necessarily involves quality assurance (7). Thus one could argue that with the emergence of qualifications frameworks, the "list of state-recognised programmes" to be published internationally for the purposes of recognition is nothing more than a "contents list" of the national qualifications framework and thus linked to national quality assurance.

1.2. A statement confirming quality

The main guarantee that the "recognition community" needs from its quality assurance counterpart is a simple and reliable statement confirming the quality behind the foreign qualification in question.

In the case of national qualifications, such a statement could confirm national approval of the qualification (programme) in question, be it accreditation or another judgment based on assessment.

In future it could constitute a statement confirming that inclusion of the qualification in question into the national qualifications framework of the awarding country has involved quality assurance and the national qualifications framework that in turn meets the compatibility criteria with the European overarching qualifications framework (7).

1.3. Mutual trust

Another important issue relates to the mutual trust between national quality assurance systems. Given the wide diversity of higher education systems and institutions there can be differences in quality standards between qualifications bearing similar names. In the "Bologna area", which has been extended to 45 countries, there is always room for the assumption that there may be differences in quality. But while it is easy to say that there may be differences in quality it is quite something else actually to prove them ultimately to assist in decisions concerning recognition.

Although international legal documents on recognition mention substantial differences in the quality of provision as one of the potential reasons for partial recognition or non-recognition of a foreign qualification, in practice it is a very delicate issue. Recognition specialists may have experience-based opinions about the quality of provision in other countries, yet it is not up to them to make judgments on the quality.

Thus, for the recognition specialists it is extremely important that the quality assurance agencies co-operate, that they themselves are assessed (if possible, internationally) and that they trust each other and can therefore supply the recognition counterpart with reliable information on quality.

In the Bergen Communiqué (6), ministers requested that co-operation among national quality assurance systems be strengthened with a view to enhancing mutual recognition of accreditation or quality assurance decisions and assessment of quality assurance agencies that should be organised nationally but involve international peers. Such developments will be highly beneficial for cross-border recognition of qualifications.

The idea of a European register of trustworthy quality assurance agencies welcomed by the ministers in their Bergen Communiqué is currently being further developed. Such a register is seen by recognition specialists as a promising development. Yet, the actual establishment of such a register is likely to happen only after the next ministerial meeting in London in May 2007.

As regards the co-operation of the agencies with a view to improving mutual recognition of quality assurance decisions, an interesting activity so far has been the one by the

European Accreditation Consortium[38] (ECA) formed by the accreditation agencies in Austria, Germany, the Flemish Community of Belgium, Ireland, the Netherlands, Norway, Spain and Switzerland. The ECA aims at mutual recognition of accreditation decisions made by the ECA member agencies (7). In 2005 some of the ECA members went even further by signing a joint declaration (8) whereby they set conditions for automatic recognition of qualifications based upon mutual recognition of accreditation decisions. The development is interesting and positive, yet it is difficult to imagine that the practice could be easily spread among all the 45 "Bologna" countries in the foreseeable future, especially because a number of countries have introduced either quality assessment systems without accreditation or use institutional rather than programme accreditation.

1.4. Cross-border qualifications

The recognition of cross-border qualifications is one of the most difficult recognition issues. Cross-border provision is a growing phenomenon and the further development of the technical means for distance provision is stimulating it. While the legal framework for recognition has been extended to cover this need through the adoption of the UNESCO/Council of Europe Code of Good Practice in the Provision of Transnational Education (9) in 2001, the main practical difficulty remains the quality assurance of the qualifications awarded across borders. There is a widespread assumption that non-serious cross-border education providers tend to avoid quality assurance and in a number of cases it may be true. However, serious cross-border education providers may be faced with the issue of access to quality assurance – on the one hand, quality assurance agencies of the sending countries may not have a duty to assess the extensions of the programmes or institutions that are located abroad, the receiving countries sometimes tend to ignore cross-border providers altogether or create rules that may make cross-border provision impossible.

One of the major needs of the recognition community from quality assurance, therefore, is co-operation between quality assurance agencies of the sending and receiving countries in the assessment of cross-border provision with a view to both making serious cross-border provision legal and possible and to eradicating fraud.

1.5. Joint degrees

Joint degrees are another area where international co-operation of quality assurance agencies is required if degrees are to be successfully recognised.

As in the case of cross-border provision, international legislation for recognition has been adapted for joint degrees – the Council of Europe/UNESCO Recommendation for the recognition of joint degrees (10) has been in place since 2004. Excellent guidelines to common quality assurance of joint programmes (11) have been prepared in terms

---

38. See more at www.ecaconsortium.net.

of the EUA Joint Master project. Yet, even more so than in the case of a "regular qualification", credential evaluators will need a reliable statement from the quality assurance side that the institutions co-operating in the delivery of the programme are recognised institutions and that all parts of the joint programme are of a trustworthy quality. The question is still open as to who can issue such a statement, as several countries and several quality assurance systems are involved. For this reason, as with "regular" degrees, in cases where actual information on quality is not available (or at least not available in such a way that it would specifically relate to the programme and qualification in question), the credential evaluators judge on the quality indirectly – asking the issuing country whether the qualification is recognised. In the case of joint degrees that actually multiplies the effort – it is important to know that all (or at least most) countries whose institutions have participated in the joint programme recognise the qualification in question.

2. Recognition of qualifications and different quality assurance models

Some of the quality assurance models with regard to recognition of individual qualifications will now be discussed.

2.1. Programme accreditation

While rightly criticised from other points of view, for example costs, high time consumption, main concentration on the status quo and weak or missing links with continuous improvement, from the point of view of recognition of individual qualifications, programme accreditation is still the type of quality assurance that provides a kind of "quality checked" label for the qualifications awarded and therefore makes it easier to make recognition decisions.

However, owing to the negative aspects mentioned above, it seems that in countries that are currently establishing quality assurance systems, the introduction of programme accreditation might not be the main trend.

2.2. Institutional accreditation or assessment

From the point of view of recognition of individual qualifications there is, in principle, no difference between institutional accreditation and other types of institutional assessment leading to a judgment that qualifies an institution as being nationally recognised.

For recognition of individual qualifications, institutional accreditation or assessment is somewhat less helpful compared to plain programme accreditation. One might expect that in the case of an accredited or positively evaluated and state-recognised higher education institution all programmes should be of a certain quality standard and enjoy recognition in the country where they are issued. This is unfortunately not always the case. In some countries the status of a "recognised institution" does not automatically imply that all the qualifications awarded by those institutions are recognised nationally. Here I refer to such countries where in parallel to programmes leading to "national" qualifications, recognised institutions can legitimately provide other programmes that do not lead to "national" qualifications but to qualifications issued "in their own name". If national authorities of these countries are asked whether such a qualification is recognised, the answer is usually negative. As a result, there is little chance that such qualifications will be recognised abroad, although the quality of the education is not necessarily poor.

This is one of the areas where co-operation between recognition and quality assurance is indeed necessary to help international recognition of valuable results of learning.

2.3. Internal quality culture of the higher education institutions

In their 2003 Berlin communiqué, the ministers (12) stated that "consistent with the principle of institutional autonomy, the primary responsibility for quality assurance in higher education lies with each institution itself". Developing an internal quality culture inside higher education institutions is being referred to as the best way to continuous quality improvement and is also proven to be less costly than, for example, the external assessment of each programme.

Yet, from the recognition point of view it is important that internal quality assurance inside the institutions is supplemented with an external assessment to provide individual qualifications with a kind of a national "quality label".

3. How far are the needs covered and what are the perspectives?

3.1. Bologna stocktaking

The Bologna stocktaking report (4) published at the Bergen ministerial conference shows huge progress towards establishing national quality assurance systems. Progress in the introduction of national systems of external quality assurance looks good and promising for the Bologna Process, especially looking into the future perspective.

For recognition needs in the "Bologna zone" the question at present centres on the current scope for full implementation of quality assurance so that credential evaluators can rely on it in their daily work. Examining the stocktaking results from this point of view shows the following: In May 2005 a fully established quality assurance system existed in 22 countries. In most other countries legislation that would result in a quality assurance system being established was at different stages of readiness for adoption and in two countries discussions related to planning for the establishment of a quality assurance system were at a preliminary stage.

As regards the important elements of quality assurance systems identified in the Berlin Communiqué (12) – internal assessment, external review, participation of students, publication of results, international participation – they have been fully implemented in 18 countries. While this is again a good sign of progress, in reality it also means that even the most basic requirement for recognition – the approval that education leading to a particular qualification is in some way quality assured – is fully met in less than half of the "Bologna zone".

3.2. EHEA standards and guidelines for quality assurance

In Bergen ministers adopted the standards and guidelines for quality assurance in the European Higher Education Area (13). It is certainly a major step forward as the standards and guidelines will be the main reference document for internal quality assurance, external assessment and assessment of the quality assurance agencies. To facilitate further development of quality assurance systems, the ministers in their Bergen Communiqué (6) requested that progress in implementation of the standards and guidelines for quality assurance should be included in the stocktaking exercise for 2007.

From the text of the standards and guidelines (13) one could conclude that the main actors in quality assurance of the programmes will be the higher education institutions themselves rather than the external reviewers. The guidelines for quality assurance of programmes are quite detailed within the part devoted to internal quality assurance while the external assessment seems to serve as an instrument for the monitoring of institutional procedures and, hopefully, providing national confirmation of their quality for international use.

In any case, implementation of the standards and guidelines will increase transparency, stimulate the move towards mutual recognition of accreditation or other decisions resulting from quality assurance and improve access to information on quality needed for recognition of qualifications.

3.3. Qualifications frameworks

The creation of national qualifications frameworks is a new phenomenon for most of the countries involved in the Bologna Process. The most visible effect of introducing national qualifications frameworks is switching to descriptions of qualifications in terms of learning outcomes and linking them to each other using the nationally defined levels. Yet, including each particular qualification into the national qualifications framework should be done through a transparent procedure involving quality assurance (8). Such a procedure would ensure that the qualifications are properly described in terms of learning outcomes and that the stipulated learning outcomes are actually achieved, thus helping recognition of individual qualifications.

3.4. Co-operation between accreditation and recognition agencies

This activity, which started recently and involves several accreditation agencies that are members of the European Consortium for Accreditation (ECA) and the ENIC/

NARIC recognition centres of the same countries, is interesting and promising. Based on both the trust in the results of (mutually recognised) accreditation and on the recognition specialists' knowledge of the higher education systems, it could indeed be possible to estimate the eventual position of the other countries' qualifications vis-à-vis one's own qualifications.

Such an exercise, however, requires a high degree of bilateral co-operation, which, if extended to the whole European Higher Education Area, might become a Sisyphean task.

Co-operation among the accreditation and recognition agencies indeed could and should lead to "automatic" recognition of qualifications in the sense that the quality and the level of qualifications is considered as recognised. In such cases further individual assessment carried out by the recognition specialists will have to establish whether or not the particular foreign qualification has substantial differences from the home prototype with regard to the purpose for which the applicant wishes to have his/her qualification recognised.

4. Summary

The needs of recognition with a view of quality assurance are well known and taken into consideration in the quality assurance community.

First of all, fair recognition of qualifications across the European Higher Education Area is only possible if there is sufficient information on the quality behind the qualifications. This means that fair recognition of qualifications needs full implementation of quality assurance across the EHEA. Statements of good quality as such are needed but what is also required is trust in these statements. Therefore, co-operation among quality assurance systems, the assessment of quality assurance agencies and finally a register of trustworthy quality agencies will promote recognition.

It is important that any programme or institution, either national, cross-border or jointly established by several national systems, has access to a fair quality assessment with a view to recognition of qualifications awarded.

Where the national quality assurance is mainly based upon the internal quality culture of its higher education institutions, a national review confirming the quality for international use is still needed.

And finally – the more quality assurance and recognition specialists communicate and co-operate, the greater chances of the holders of individual qualifications being fairly recognised.

References

(1) Divis J., International recognition and quality assurance – two priorities of Bologna, paper presented at the official Bologna seminar "Improving the recognition system", Riga, 3-4 December 2004, www.aic.lv/rigaseminar/documents/Divis_paper.pdf

(2) Council of Europe/UNESCO Convention on the Recognition of Qualifications Concerning Higher Education in the European Region, Lisbon, 11 April 1997, www.ace/ace_disk/Recognition/leg_aca/Lisb_con.pdf

(3) Council of Europe/UNESCO Recommendation on Criteria and Procedures for the Assessment of Foreign Qualifications, adopted 6 June 2001, www.aic.lv/ace/ace_disk/Recognition/leg_aca/Recom.pdf

(4) Bologna Process stocktaking. Report to the Bergen ministerial conference, Bergen, 2005, www.bologna-bergen2005.no/Bergen/050509_Stocktaking.pdf

(5) Adam S., Final report of the conference "Improving the recognition system of degrees and study credit points in the European Higher Education Area", Riga, 3-4 December 2004, www.aic.lv/ ace/ace_disk/Bologna/Bol_semin/Riga/04120304_Riga_Report.pdf

(6) The European Higher Education Area – Achieving the Goals. Communiqué of the Conference of European Ministers responsible for Higher Education, Bergen, 19-20 May 2005, www.bologna-bergen2005.no/Docs/00-Main_doc/050520_Bergen_Communique.pdf

(7) ECA Agreement of Co-operation, see www.ecaconsortium.net/download.php?id=22

(8) Bologna working group on Qualifications frameworks. A framework of qualifications for the European Higher Education Area. ISBN 87-91469-54-6, Copenhagen, 2005, cf. pp. 8, 48-51, 75-88

(9) UNESCO/ Council of Europe Code of Good Practice in the Provision of Transnational Education, adopted in 2001, www.aic.lv/ace/ace_disk/Recognition/leg_aca/CodeTE.pdf

(10) Council of Europe/UNESCO Recommendation on the recognition of joint degrees, Adopted 9 June 2004, www.aic.lv/ace/ace_disk/Recognition/leg_aca/RecJDand_ExpM.pdf

(11) European University Association. Guidelines for quality enhancement in European Joint master programmes, 2006, p. 30, www.eua.be/eua/jsp/en/upload/EMNEM_report.1147364824803.pdf

(12) Realising the European Higher Education Area. Communiqué of the Conference of Ministers responsible for Higher Education in Berlin on 19 September 2003, www.bologna-berlin2003.de/en/communique_minister/index.htm

(13) "Standards and guidelines for quality assurance in the European Higher Education Area". European Association for Quality Assurance in Higher Education, Helsinki, 2005, www.bologna-bergen2005.no/Docs/00-Main_doc/050221_ENQA_report.pdf

The use of outcomes of quality assurance

Norman Sharp

The Council of Europe Forum for Higher Education has provided us with a very well-constructed programme round the issues of legitimacy of quality assurance and the role of public authorities and institutions. We have heard in the opening presentation from Luc Weber about approaches to, and rationales for, quality assurance in higher education in Europe. We have also been led in discussion by Alberto Amaral and Ossi V. Lindqvist on the roles and responsibilities of public authorities and institutions. In addition to the excellent exemplars provided during the conference, the panel discussion focused on the central issue of winning acceptance for quality assurance. The forum is to be congratulated on providing a platform for discussing these important and, I believe, closely inter-related matters. In many conferences and discussions in Europe on quality matters the focus of discussions on quality assurance is frequently on the "how?" questions:

- How can we devise efficient and effective, valid and reliable systems for review at subject level?
- for review at the institutional level?
- for the allocation of credit points and levels to our degrees and course units?

Essentially, in this chapter I would like to change the focus from the "how?" and "who?" questions to discuss the "why?" question. I would like to begin by outlining my simple thesis and then go on to illustrate the implications of this thesis by discussing four key outcomes of thinking differently about the role of quality assurance systems. My thesis is essentially in three parts. First I will argue that we can only understand and deliver effectively in respect of the "how" and "who" questions once we have understood, in our own particular social, economic and political contexts, the "why" question. Second, I will argue that a focus on educational excellence will, to a significant extent, meet the other imperatives behind the drive for quality assurance. Third, I will argue that the impact of quality assurance processes will be maximised when the outcomes of the quality assurance systems themselves become inputs, and we move into the virtuous circle of quality enhancement.

Why?

First, then, the importance of the why? question. I participated recently in a discussion on quality assurance with colleagues in Chile. During these discussions Professor Henrik Montenegro posed a very interesting question for all of us involved in the business of quality assurance. He asked, "When we look back in ten years'time, what will have changed as a result of our efforts? Will we look back and say that we have devised sophisticated processes, efficient review structures, clever audit methodologies, processes that ran increasingly smoothly? Or, will we be able say that we have contributed to a real impact on the quality of the student experience?" It seems to me that Professor Montenegro was getting to the heart of the why? question. While there are clearly other issues involved, the heart of the matter must surely be the impact we have, directly and indirectly, on the quality of the student experience.

However, as we have discussed during the forum, when you ask the why? question there will be many varied answers from different perspectives. The specific focus of our answer will depend on our particular frame (or frames) of reference. There are three very commonly used frames of reference which are by no means mutually exclusive:

- market failure;
- public accountability;
- educational excellence.

In the first of these, the rationale for intervention in relation to quality assurance is based on the failure of the market. From this perspective it is argued that, in a perfect market, the free choice of well-informed and frequent consumers would drive out poor quality and support the growth of efficient and effective high-quality institutions. The evidence is, of course, very clear: the higher education "market" does not operate in this way. The market cannot be relied on to provide secure quality assurance, let alone quality enhancement arrangements. In the jargon of the economist, we have neither perfectly informed and frequent "consumers" nor a structure of perfectly competitive "producers". The second line of argument is that all education, including higher education, is a public good which directly and indirectly involves significant sums of public money and these aspects bring with them a requirement for public accountability. It is argued that, because of vested interest, the institutions themselves operating freely cannot be relied on to meet the requirements of public accountability, and that we, therefore, require some form of external intervention in relation to the assurance of quality and standards. The third line of argument is based on the importance of quality assurance arrangements in supporting the delivery of educational excellence given the fundamental importance of higher education in securing individual, community and economic wellbeing and prosperity. As I indicated a moment ago, these three perspectives are not mutually exclusive and indeed in many areas are closely inter-related. Some matters of public accountability in themselves will derive from aspects of market failure, and issues of public accountability will, in general, be closely related to matters of educational excellence.

The pre-eminence of educational excellence

The second part of my thesis follows exactly from the above: to a significant extent, if we focus our attention appropriately on striving to achieve educational excellence, the requirements of public accountability and the problems posed by market failure will be largely addressed. An institution that seriously and effectively internalises a drive for educational excellence in the experience offered to its students will not be able to coast on a sea of inadequacy supported by its monopolistic position even if it was tempted to do so. Equally, the institution with effective quality enhancement strategies in place will be in a position to meet the requirements of public accountability by always striving in systematic ways to deliver educational excellence. I would argue in this context that the public security that would be required should be the guarantee that there are effective quality management systems in place.

The virtuous circle of quality enhancement

The third and final part of my thesis is that, in general, the power of the outcomes of quality assurance is maximised when the outputs of the quality assurance systems themselves become inputs and we move into the virtuous circles of quality enhancement. That is, we manage quality, not for its own sake, but rather we explicitly manage quality in order to enhance the experience offered to the students and communities we seek to serve. It is important that our higher education institutions should reflect carefully on the evidence of past performance in order to gain insight into past performance, and audit trails of course committees, student surveys and graduation/employment rates are all helpful and important. However, this is the beginning of effective quality management, not the end point. The key question is now, "so what?" Is this good, bad or indifferent? Against what national and international benchmarks are we comparing ourselves? How does this compare with emerging good practice in teaching and learning? Where does this indicate we need, either as an individual institution, or collectively as a higher education sector, to invest some development resource? What good practice can we pass from one department, faculty or school to another? In other words, the outcomes of our quality processes are providing the evidential base for prioritising improvement: the outcomes become a key input into our quality enhancement strategy. In subsequent rounds of the quality cycle, evidence is then available on the effectiveness or otherwise of change and so the process continues, and we are into the virtuous circle of quality enhancement. Essentially, this is true at the level of the individual department, faculty and institution, and, potentially, at the level of the sector. My argument, briefly, is that to be effective, a quality management system must be a double-sided coin: assurance and enhancement. Enhancement processes must be based on firm evidence of the base we are working from. Equally, experience tells us that assurance processes that are not linked to enhancement fall rapidly into neglect, game playing and/or sterile box-ticking exercises.

Summary

In summary, my simple thesis is:

- in relation to quality management, the who? and how? questions can only be addressed meaningfully once we have answered the why? question;
- the why? question is most effectively answered from the perspective of "educational excellence" which, to a significant extent, will address the challenges posed by public accountability and market failure;

- the impact of quality assurance processes will be maximised when the outcomes of the quality assurance systems themselves become inputs and we move into the virtuous circle of quality enhancement.

If colleagues are interested in pursuing these matters further, a more detailed analysis along similar lines is provided in the report published by the Scottish Executive, "Learning to improve: quality approaches to lifelong learning".[39]

In the sections that follow I will apply aspects of my thesis to four strategic macro-level outcomes from thinking differently about quality management.

Outcome 1: a shared vision (within a system/country) of a high-quality sector

Let us start with a tautology. Before we can provide any effective management of quality in relation to a particular system or country, we need to know what our target is: what is the definition of a high-quality higher education sector within our system or country? As a pre-requisite to having effective quality management arrangements in place, I would argue, for example, that all 45 Bologna process countries would need to be involved, in their own ways, in answering this question. It may well be that, over time, there will be more shared aspects of the definition of high quality over the Bologna countries, as to some extent is apparent in the work of ENQA outlined earlier in the conference by its President, Peter Williams.[40] In general, how the question is answered and who answers the question will of course vary widely from country to country. In some highly market-oriented systems where there is little public funding in higher education it may well be that this sector-wide definition of high quality is fairly loose. In other contexts it will be a much tighter definition of quality. It is worth noting in the margins that this is not directly a function of institutional autonomy or its lack; it is perfectly possible, as in Scotland, to have highly autonomous institutions that collectively agree on a sector-wide vision of "high quality". Any definition is likely to change and develop over time and to result from the interplay of the range of stakeholders. Notwithstanding the complexities involved, it seems to me that, if there is to be an effective framework of national policy in relation to quality assurance and enhancement, it is vital that there is clarity in sense of purpose: that is, what kind of higher education system are we seeking to provide? My own experience would suggest that the more participatory the exercise of defining high quality, the more powerful will be the outcome. Such a sector- or system-wide definition of high quality will then set a general context within which the mission and policies of each individual institution will be derived. The more explicit and shared the sector-wide vision, the more powerful the outcome: the more implicit and widely contested, the shakier the foundations for any system of quality assurance. Before moving on to

---

39. "Learning to improve: quality approaches to lifelong learning", Scottish Executive, Edinburgh 2005.
40. Standards and Guidelines for Quality Assurance in the European Higher Education Area, European Association for Quality Assurance in Higher Education, Helsinki, 2005.

provide an illustration of this outcome, let me re-state my view that, used effectively, this outcome should support both institutional diversity and institutional autonomy.

Box 1 below provides an illustration of one attempt at deriving a country-wide vision of high quality in Scotland: a context in which the higher educational institutions are highly autonomous.

Box 1: A country-wide vision of high quality

In Scotland, over the period 1999-2001 there was a sector-wide discussion involving the 20 institutions, their students and various stakeholders on the meaning of a high-quality sector. This rich and valuable debate resulted in the vision that a high-quality sector was:

– a sector which is flexible, accessible and responsive to the needs of learners, the economy and society,

– a sector which encourages and stimulates learners to participate in higher education and to achieve their full potential,

– a sector where learning and teaching promote the employability of students,

– a sector where learning and teaching are highly regarded and appropriately resourced,

– a sector where there is a culture of continuous enhancement of quality, which is informed by and contributes to international developments.

Outcome 2: a shared vision of high quality within an institution

For brevity I will not repeat much of what I have said above, which is also highly relevant in the context of deriving an internal vision of high quality within an institution. Effective management of quality requires that an institution (and its staff) understands itself and that it has a clear picture of what, in its own terms, are the characteristics of a high-quality institution. Such a definition, to be effective, should clearly be derived by the institution in relation to the needs of its particular students and the needs of other populations it serves. As with Outcome 1 above, the more explicit and shared this vision, the more powerful the impact of the outcome: the more implicit and contested, the shakier will be the foundations on which to build any system of quality assurance.

Box 2 below provides an example of the mission of one university which clearly places significant emphasis on excellence in teaching and serving its community. It is interesting to note in passing that the immediate neighbourhood of this particular institution includes areas of very significant social deprivation.

Box 2: An institution-wide vision of high quality

The following example provides an interesting illustration of one institution's approach to defining high quality:

- mission: to be a regional, innovative and inclusive university with strong national and international links committed to excellence in teaching, knowledge transfer and research and to serving the social, cultural and economic needs of the regional communities it serves.

Two main drivers for delivering the mission:

- planned strategic approaches to anticipate and respond to the needs of the students it recruits,
- a structured process of continuous review and reflection on current practice and provision.

This is delivered through an integrated organisational structure involving:

- Quality Enhancement Unit,
- Senate Committee – the Learning and Teaching Board – linked to other structures throughout the university,
- the Vice-Principal (Learning and Teaching) managing and overseeing the process.

This is further supported by:

- a structured and explicit approach to student engagement,
- a strong research basis on their students, their learning styles and support needs,
- on-going systems evaluation to underpin further development and quality enhancement.

Outcome 3: supporting students as effective, demanding lifelong learners

In many ways it seems to me that this is the most fundamental outcome of all: indeed, as argued above, the *raison d'être* of quality assurance systems. There are many different dimensions of "high quality" which are not central to this particular discussion, and therefore I will not dwell on them. Much could be said, for example, about the importance of learning outcomes. These are indeed vital – vital for clarity of purpose, for relevance and validity of assessment instruments and pedagogical approaches, and for the recognition of prior learning. However, I would like to focus in this chapter on what is probably the most fundamental aspect of quality assurance: the function of quality assurance systems in supporting the learner, and consequently, the role of learners in these processes. In general, we are successful, to a greater or lesser extent across most European countries, in getting feedback from our students following their studies – at programme, course and institutional level. This is important, and there is a growing body of evidence now available to us on more and less effective approaches to getting and using this student feedback. This much is relatively uncontentious, well understood and documented. I would like, however, to look at a different aspect of student engagement – supporting the effective learning of students in higher education. To do this, I would like to spend just a very brief moment reflecting on the nature of learning in higher education.

In this section of the presentation I will draw heavily on the work of John Biggs, who I think summarises very helpfully many of these issues in his excellent book, *Teaching for Quality Learning at University*.[41] Let's start with a very basic question: What do we mean by "high-quality teaching" in higher education? It seems to Biggs that one of the defining features of higher education is the engagement of students in the process by which knowledge is created. In other words, students, even first-year students at university, should be exposed to the temporary nature of knowledge. Our understanding of the world and of our particular academic discipline has arrived at its current state through a process of knowledge creation. This process will continue over time, and the boundaries of knowledge will continue to get pushed beyond that which we currently understand. This is true for all disciplines: only the methodology of discovery varies. It seems to me that this simple premise lies at the heart of what is sometimes referred to as research-led teaching. This is simply an approach to learning which introduces students to the notion of discovery: how that discovery comes about, and understanding the tools of discovery. This in turn lays the foundations for students as graduates who will become lifelong learners, and effective, over their lifetimes, in the workplace and in their communities. If these outcomes are to be achieved, the student must engage in what Biggs and other writers refer to as deep learning. Deep learning is contrasted with surface learning, the latter being at the other end of the spectrum from the process of knowledge creation. Biggs describes surface learning as engaging in such activities as memorising, identifying things, naming things, paraphrasing, enumerating and describing. On the other hand, deep learning is characterised by activities such as: reflecting; applying to novel problems; hypothesising; relating new information to principles; arguing; and comparing and contrasting a range of perspectives.

The question then arises, how is an institution and an individual academic going to encourage deep learning? How is a mature institution going to continually enhance the student learning experience? How are we going to approach the task of quality assurance of the teaching/learning process? The brief answer to this, according to Biggs, is that the institution must become an enhancing institution. By this he means that the institution requires to develop a reflective culture that builds in systemic ways of reflecting, together

---

41. Biggs, J., *Teaching for Quality Learning at University*, 2nd edn, Society for Research into Higher Education and Open University Press, Buckingham, England, 2003.

with its students, on the effectiveness of learning experiences and how these experiences might be improved. By reflecting on what the evidence indicates, the institution, and its various sub-structures, will be led to develop further refinements, and so enter the "virtuous circle" of quality enhancement referred to earlier.

The next part of the jigsaw is then to relate our analysis of learning to thinking about approaches to teaching. Biggs describes three different approaches which, he argues, might be thought of as successive steps taken by academics as they approach the task of teaching, progressing from novice to expert. The first stage he describes as focusing on the student. The caricature here is the academic preparing excellent material for lectures or tutorials. If the student fails to learn, then the problem is seen to lie with the student – the students are ill-prepared, or lazy, or poorly motivated, or "not as bright as they used to be". In this approach, the teacher is the knowledgeable expert who expounds the information, and the students' task is to absorb and report back accurately what they have "learned" from the teacher. Teaching therefore becomes focused on the transmission of information, and it is entirely up to the students whether they receive or don't receive this information. The role of the teacher is to transmit. The role of quality assurance would be to quality-assure the transmission.

The second approach Biggs caricatures as "the tool box" approach. In this context staff will think carefully about the different ways in which teaching might be undertaken: choosing the right tool for the job. New lecturer induction courses will be designed to expose staff to the different tools available and how they might be deployed effectively. If there is a problem in relation to ineffective teaching, the solution is to provide better tools or more staff development to support more expert utilisation of the tools. The role of quality assurance in this context would be to assure the effectiveness and extent of the repertoire of tools deployed.

Biggs' third stage is to conceive of learning in terms of an effective partnership between the teacher and the student in the creation of the student's knowledge. It is of course not simply a relationship between the teacher and the student, but involves all of the educational resources that the institution represents, often channelled through the teacher or the individual academic. The focus here becomes a focus, not on teaching, but on learning and on what the student does in order to master learning. From this perspective, it is of course important that students are appropriately prepared, that they do have required prerequisite knowledge and that they do have accessible means for accessing new knowledge. Equally, the teaching context remains important with the effective exercise of the teaching role and responsibilities fundamental to successful learning. But, giving "good" lectures *per se* may be largely irrelevant. The key question for quality assurance is: is it supporting stet effective student learning? The task, according to Biggs, is to create a teaching context where deep learning can take place. If we are going to achieve this, then we need to achieve what the jargon terms as "constructive alignment", that is, where there is a clear alignment between the curriculum that we provide, the teaching/learning methods that we use, the assessment procedures adopted, the climate and context within which individual academics interact with their students and the institutional climate within which all of this occurs.

If we are to achieve this most challenging of outcomes, what are the implications for our quality assurance systems? The first, and, in my view, the most fundamental, is the importance of the enhancement focus which I will deal with in the final section of this chapter. The second lesson relates to the very fundamental question this raises about how we conceive of high-quality pedagogical practice and the kind of evidence we should be collecting from students, together with the kind of processes and criteria we should be putting in place for programme/course validations, monitoring and review and other quality assurance processes. However, the implication I would like to dwell on for a moment is the need to support the active role of students in all this. The simple model of quality-assuring a transmitter/receiver relationship will no longer do. Students are "joint producers" of their knowledge and must be appropriately engaged in the quality assurance of this process of knowledge creation. Therefore, a key part of the approach to achieving this most important of all outcomes is the effective involvement of students in our quality systems. From this perspective, students should be represented on all key internal committees and engaged appropriately in internal and external quality assurance structures. Fundamentally, their engagement must not be token. Students must be prepared for, and supported, in these important roles. A key element of this would be supporting students in developing appropriate learning styles, that is, reflecting on their own learning.

Box 3 below provides an illustration of the ways in which students are now involved in the Quality Enhancement Framework throughout the higher education sector in Scotland.

**Box 3: The involvement of students in quality management
in the Scottish Quality Enhancement Framework**

Since 2003 students have played an increased role in quality management throughout Scottish higher education, at both institutional and sector levels. Indeed, the current chairman of the national Quality Working Group (QWG) is the President of the National Union of Students in Scotland. The QWG brings together the institutions, students, and the national bodies associated with quality to manage the overall quality framework in Scotland.

Other elements of student involvement include:

- student representation at all levels within institutions,
- training and support for students in quality matters,
- an independent body to support effective student involvement in quality matters (SPARQS),
- student involvement in external quality processes including as full members of external review teams,
- student involvement in national strategy and policy levels on quality matters.

Outcome 4: a virtuous circle of quality enhancement

Can I start this section with an apology? I apologise for repeatedly using the term "enhancement". I share many people's hatred of jargon, and I would have to say, in particular, educational jargon. There is seldom anything more effective in turning off mainstream academics faster than reading papers or listening to presentations that are full of educational gobbledegook. However, the word "enhancement" is actually important in this context. It is not simply improvement. Enhancement implies a continuing process. It implies a process of making change, evaluating the outcomes of change, capturing the benefits of change and repeating the cycle of reflection and evidence gathering. Hence, I deliberately use the term "enhancement".

My simple thesis contends that the main outcome of institutional quality assurance strategies should be to support enhancement of the experience available to students. Enhancement, I define in this context as "taking deliberate steps to bring about continuous improvement in the effectiveness of the learning experience of students".[42] In order to take these deliberate steps, an institution (and its constituent departments, faculties, schools, etc.) will ask itself a range of questions including:

- Where are we now? How effective is the current learning experience of our students?
- Where do we want to be in the future? What are the patterns and mechanisms of supporting learning which the institution wishes to develop in order to enhance the learning experience of its students? What appropriate benchmarks should we use in this context? What countries/universities/professions. provide useful benchmarks for us to compare ourselves with?
- How are we going to get there? How are we as an institution going strategically to manage the process of enhancement that will allow us to move towards meeting our aspirations?

The first step in this process is therefore to have an accurate, evidence-based picture of the current position: without this, enhancement cannot begin. A key part of the function of internal quality assurance systems is to inform an institution about itself – the outcomes of course or programme monitoring and review, student feedback, employer feedback and so on. To collect this information and do nothing with it is largely a waste of valuable and scarce resources. The real value comes from the academic community – students and staff – asking the "so what?" question: what does all this information tell us about ourselves in relation to our aspirations? In this context, institutional quality frameworks need to use a structure of benchmarks to make comparative sense of the information they have gathered in order to interpret the outcomes of their quality assurance processes. Some of these benchmarks might well be internal to the institution (for example, institutional mission and

---

42. *Handbook for Enhancement-led Institutional Review: Scotland*, Quality Assurance Agency for Higher Education, Gloucester, 2003.

other specific internal targets): others will be country-wide (participation rates of different social groups, graduate employment statistics etc.). Some benchmarks will be shared throughout European countries; others will be shared with particular international groupings of universities. This process of benchmarking will enable an institution to evaluate its own position and decide on appropriate actions and quality objectives for the future.

The third question in the trilogy, "how are we going to get there?", is equally vital. As Peter Williams has stated, "quality improvement does not happen by accident: it is the result of intelligent effort".[43] The final part of this complex jigsaw is to analyse the "intelligent effort" of the institution: how does it manage effectively the process of quality enhancement? This is likely to involve the development of the internal culture of the institution and the alignment of its internal quality systems. For example, from this perspective, course or programme reviews should not simply be backward-looking at what has been happening in the past. They require to be forward-looking to address the question of how we can learn from the past – and experience elsewhere – to improve the future for our students. Outcomes from such processes should identify areas for development and improvement and these require to be managed institutionally to provide the means for delivering on this improvement. For example:

- staff support and development activities need to be aligned explicitly with the outcomes of institutional quality systems and targets;
- at an institutional and/or system level, whatever resources are available should be systematically channelled into addressing areas recognised to be difficult across the institution/and or across the country or system.

Box 4 below provides a final example of one attempt to achieve this outcome. It outlines the main headings of the Quality Enhancement Framework in Scotland which, in this particular form, has been in operation since 2003. It is based on a number of key principles including:

- enhancement: the framework is explicitly enhancement-focused: not at the cost of assurance, but building on the foundations of assurance;
- partnership: the institutions, students, funding council (with government accountability) and Quality Assurance Agency have developed the framework in partnership and regularly review it, together with the effectiveness of its operation. The independence of each party remains respected and protected;
- student-centred: the framework is focused on enhancing the student learning experience – systems are a means to an end, not an end in themselves;
- evaluation: the framework has been subject systematically to both internal and external evaluation from the outset and consequent fine-tuning of processes.

---

43. Quoted from a conference address by Peter Williams, Chief Executive QAA, President ENQA.

Box 4: The Scottish Quality Enhancement Framework

The Scottish Quality Enhancement Framework was introduced in 2003. It emerged following a full cycle of external subject-level reviews and a complete cycle of institutional quality audits. It was the result of wide discussion and reflection on the outcomes of previous processes and evidence available on effective approaches to quality management. The key principles are outlined above. Central elements of the Quality Enhancement Framework include:

- subject-level reviews conducted by the institutions themselves, but involving externals, student feedback and production of full reports which are available to the Quality Assurance Agency;
- the involvement of students at all levels within higher education institutions on committees related to the quality of the student experience;
- additional training and support for students in quality matters provided by an independent body (SPARQS);
- a programme of national enhancement themes on topics identified by the sector as involving particular challenges in improving the student experience. Within the themes a wide range of development, workshop and dissemination activities are undertaken, drawing on national and international expertise and experience. Topics covered to date include: assessment; employability; and flexible learning. Current themes are the first-year experience and research teaching links;
- a programme of external enhancement-led institutional review (ELIR), which provides both public accountability for institutional management of quality and support for institutional management of quality enhancement. This is a peer review process with a student as a full member of each review team. This process is described fully in the published ELIR Handbook.

Conclusions

I am very conscious that I have touched very lightly on some very heavy topics. My purpose has been simply to place some of the fundamental aspects of quality processes in a significantly different context from that in which they are frequently placed. In order to think constructively about the role of different players in relation to quality and to plan quality systems, it is vital, in my view, first of all to reflect on the question why? – what is the purpose of all this? I have attempted to argue for the pre-eminence of the driving force of quality enhancement: to enhance the quality of the experience of the students and communities our institutions serve. That is not to say that other ends are not important: they clearly are. However, the probability of achieving these other ends, I would argue, is greater to the extent we are successful in enhancing the experience of our students. In general, I have attempted to argue that the rewards of investing in quality systems will be the richer, the more these systems are forward-looking and enhancement-focused, rather than backward-looking and focused on sterile box-ticking exercises. I have tried to argue briefly that the achievement of these outcomes will maximise the probability of autonomous universities serving our countries by creating individuals who are: effective lifelong learners; productive, dynamic and mobile members of the workforce; and, perhaps most importantly, engaged citizens of Europe.

The legitimacy of quality assurance

The role of public authorities and institutions: towards conclusions and recommendations

Lewis Purser

1. Introduction

Enhancing the quality of European higher education at institutional, national and European levels has been among the key issues of the Bologna process from the very beginning. In the rapidly changing environment of higher education, the provision and maintenance of high quality and standards in higher education institutions have likewise become a major concern for higher education institutions themselves and for public authorities.

The Council of Europe's Steering Committee for Higher Education and Research therefore organised a higher education forum on the theme "The Legitimacy of Quality Assurance in Higher Education: the Role of Public Authorities and Institutions". This forum was held at the Council of Europe's headquarters in Strasbourg on 19-20 September 2006, in co-operation with the European Association for Quality Assurance in Higher Education (ENQA) and the European University Association (EUA). The forum brought together approximately 90 senior decision-makers from higher education ministries, quality assurance agencies, higher education institutions, and representative bodies across Europe. It was specifically designed to co-ordinate with the quality forum being organised in Munich in November 2006 by EUA in co-operation with ENQA, ESIB (the National Unions of Students in Europe) and EURASHE (the European Association of Higher Education Institutions).

The higher education forum was dedicated to the memory of Stefanie Hofmann, vice-president of ENQA, who had been a member of the forum planning committee, and of Roland Vermeesch, secretary general of EURASHE. Both were central figures in European higher education and passed away in most untimely circumstances earlier in 2006.

Rather than discuss the general principles of quality assurance, the forum focused on the relationship between quality assurance, the public responsibility for higher education and research, and higher education governance. Through the exploration of different understandings and practices of quality assurance in a variety of European countries and settings, the forum was able to examine the roles and responsibilities of the public authorities in quality assurance, and to consider elements important for the legitimacy and acceptance of quality assurance methods and results by higher education institutions, students and staff, as well as by broader society.

The following report is based on the presentations made during the forum and the rich discussion and debate which accompanied these. The full texts of the different individual presentations are available elsewhere in this publication. This report attempts to bring together the most pertinent ideas of each element of the forum into a reasonably coherent whole.

2. Public responsibility

The responsibility for well-functioning and productive higher education and research systems in most European countries has traditionally been a public one, at least since the middle of the 20th century. This has been based on the notion that there are major collective returns on public investment in these areas. These returns extend also to those who do not benefit directly from participation in higher education, but who derive secondary benefits from living in a highly educated society.

However, the ever-increasing economic competition between countries and regions resulting from globalisation means that quality assurance in higher education now assumes higher levels of importance than was previously the case. One implication of this has been the necessity for European societies continuously to renovate their systems of higher education and research in order to surmount new economic and social challenges. The quality of these services provided by higher education institutions is therefore central.

The traditional European concept of equal opportunity has likewise contributed to a sense of public responsibility for higher education. This is linked to the contribution of higher education to social and cultural enrichment, cohesion and sustainability. This historical commitment is matched by a renewed commitment to this public responsibility, made collectively by European ministers in 2001 at their Bologna process summit in Prague.

2.1. Quality assurance

Given this public responsibility for higher education, it therefore follows that there should also be some overall level of public responsibility for quality assurance in higher education. There are a number of reasons for this.

The first is that there are high levels of public investment in higher education and research in European countries. Although academics, students and higher education institutions, and in some cases broader society also, often complain that this public investment is insufficient, it is nevertheless substantial in both relative and real terms. It is therefore necessary to ensure the relevance and effectiveness of this investment, particularly if it is desirable to increase the overall scale of this investment.

The second is that, unlike the private sector, there is no automatic and effective system of sanctions and rewards in the public sector. This means that the mechanisms which rule in the private sector are not as relevant in public higher education, and points to the legitimacy of state intervention to regulate markets.

A third reason is that higher education is not a typical commercial good. It has a number of unusual features which reinforce the need for some form of public responsibility to protect the interests of learners. The problem of ensuring adequate "market" information for potential "buyers" is acute, since with higher education you only know what you have bought once you have started to "consume" it. Higher education is likewise considered a "rare purchase", in many cases only made once during a lifetime, so the consumer is unable to adjust his/her behaviour accordingly, based on previous experience, in order to buy a different product next time, since there may be no "next time". Furthermore there are high opt-out costs to higher education, meaning that it is difficult to change choices once these have been made. Added to these, the majority of higher education students could be considered as immature consumers, in economic terms, whose choices are not always rational. In such cases, it may be more effective for the state, or an agent of the state, rather than the individual consumer, to deal directly with the provider in terms of negotiating and ensuring satisfactory levels of service. It is usually the case that the state can get a better bargain on behalf of collective consumer needs than any one individual.

A fourth reason in favour of public responsibility for quality assurance is that the collective effort to establish the European higher education and research area demands trust across different higher education systems. This trust must be grounded in robust and transparent quality assurance procedures, and the importance of each national quality assurance system for other European countries therefore becomes greater. Some level of public responsibility for these is needed to ensure that this trust is not misplaced.

History has consistently shown that autonomous higher education institutions are more likely to be successful in working towards their own multi-faceted and complex missions than those institutions which are managed in an interventionist fashion by the public authorities. Without this autonomy institutions are unable to respond flexibly and in innovative ways to the needs of society and to new opportunities. And without such autonomy, institutions will not be able to compete. However, when they do compete, it is not guaranteed that they will consistently pursue the public good. In difficult economic circumstances, non-profit organisations – including universities – tend to behave like for-profit ones. The state therefore still needs to maintain a certain level of oversight to ensure the fulfilment of policy objectives.

2.2. Different approaches

The public responsibility for quality assurance in Europe is currently manifest in a number of different ways. These differences reflect to a certain extent different cultural approaches to higher education and quality assurance, and also the relative maturity and experience of these systems. The approaches taken to quality assurance by individual higher education systems and the public authorities will also change over time, and there are many instances across Europe of such change over the last ten years.

One first such difference is the extent to which this responsibility reaches into all areas of the higher education system. In some countries, the state restricts its oversight to public institutions only, while in others this oversight is explicitly extended to private higher education institutions also. In both cases, the state needs to ensure that each institution's internal quality assurance systems are periodically evaluated, and has a duty to provide information to students and families about the quality of institutions and programmes. However, some traditionally minded actors still regard such state intervention in quality assurance as symptomatic of a lack of trust, and leading to concepts such as new public management. In their perspective, quality assurance risks being reduced to the concept of responding to client needs and ensuring client satisfaction.

A second set of differences surround the definition of public responsibility for quality assurance as a choice between formative or summative methodologies. Either of these choices will greatly influence behaviour by the higher education institutions affected, since the outcomes in either case are rather different. A formative approach offers the perspective of providing encouragement and support for improvement and enhancement, whereas a summative approach is primarily concerned with a yes/no answer concerning a set of minimum requirements, to which sanctions can be added as appropriate.

These choices could also be summarised as being qualitative or quantitative approaches. However, a quantitative approach requires that we have objective indicators which are valid (and have the same values and meanings) for all institutions, which is often difficult to achieve even within the same higher education system, let alone across a number of European countries. A softer qualitative approach demands that institutions should open up and be transparent in the same spirit as the formative approach mentioned above. However, the effectiveness of this approach depends to a great deal on the professionalism and independence of evaluators.

A further set of possible variations in how public responsibility operates concerns the focus of quality assurance mechanisms. There have traditionally been many varied approaches across Europe concerning standards, programmes, institutions or a combination of these. This variety of focus is based on different perspectives of how to ensure that each individual student's qualification is of sufficient quality to be recognised across Europe. This has in many cases provided the rationale for programme accreditation. However, with the massive expansion of higher education in recent decades and the increasing variety and flexibility of study programmes, many now consider it unrealistic to certify all programmes across Europe – a process which would take decades and which cannot, in most cases, respond rapidly to the need for regular changes in these programmes. Indeed many national quality assurance systems have been moving from a programme-based approach to an institutional approach to quality. As part of this re-focusing, the responsibility of institutions for quality assurance is emphasised, including taking responsibility for the quality of individual students' qualifications so that these can be used both at home and abroad by graduates.

2.3. Impact

Given all these factors, it is also relevant and interesting to look at the impact of these quality assurance exercises so far. However, from what can be observed across the different approaches to quality assurance, there has only been a limited impact so far in any one field. This can partly be explained by the fact that, whatever the approaches currently in use, quality assurance systems in many parts of Europe could still be said to be in a state of adolescence. Only a handful of national quality assurance agencies are more than twenty years old, and most are considerably younger.

The impact of accreditation is mitigated by the fact that the numbers of programmes and institutions which have been through an accreditation process but which have not been accredited are very low. Given the huge efforts undertaken by all involved in such processes, and the on-going policy discourse regarding the need for more effective and efficient higher education, this is somewhat disappointing. Does this imply that the standards have been set too low, or that the process has not been robust enough to identify programmes which are in fact weak? The question should also be asked whether we want to create a European higher education area where every institution and/or programme simply achieves minimum standards, or whether these levels of acceptable quality should suit the profiles of each institution and/or programme, with rigorous mechanisms in place to assure this.

Conversely, however, the impact of improvement-led evaluations is lessened in many cases by the lack of suitable follow-up mechanisms. This follow-up phase has typically been the weakest link in this approach, and indeed has sometimes been completely forgotten. Such follow-up mechanisms require the development of enhancement plans, with concrete steps to ensure these measures are financed and that monitoring arrangements are put in place. However, in recent years, a number of the more established quality assurance systems, for example in Finland, have now explicitly become improvement oriented, where follow-up is an essential part of the quality enhancement process.

A third area where the impact of quality assurance needs to be examined is its capacity to promote strategic behaviour and change. Are the essential issues which ought to be covered in fact being addressed during the evaluation process? Or are they conveniently being ignored? How have the outcomes of quality assurance activities influenced broader strategic management and planning issues for the higher education institution in question?

A further area where the potential impact of quality assurance is as yet unclear is when the entire evaluation process begins to operate more as a well-oiled administrative machine, where the key motivations of learning and improvement are in danger of being replaced by that of minimal impact and – for those acting as "expert" peers in the process – the attraction of financial reward is greater than the learning opportunities afforded by the unique privilege of being invited to observe and comment on the core activities of an institution for higher education and research. Such shifts change fundamentally the experiences of all involved, and the prime objective of enhancing quality at the institution in question can no longer be said to be valid.

One area of potential impact which is often ignored is whether the increase in quality assurance activity has improved the capacity of students to make rational choices when deciding about their own learning pathways. Evidence for this is patchy across Europe, and experience related during the forum from Portugal and the Netherlands would suggest that many undergraduate students, at least in their early years in higher education, rely on unofficial sources of information from family and friends when making choices, rather than on more formal sources from government, the media or the higher education institutions themselves. Such information is then linked to other criteria such as distance from home, an attractive environment, and other relevant personal preferences. The real influence of quality assurance on these student choices is therefore at best limited.

2.4. European dimension

There is a rapidly growing European dimension to the public responsibility for quality assurance. Apart from the ongoing developments in this area as part of the Bologna process, the opening of the European labour market and the daily social, economic and cultural realities for citizens in today's Europe all mean that the relevance of this enhanced European dimension is becoming increasingly important.

One central element of this European dimension is being able to co-ordinate national quality assurance systems across borders, in order to maximise the benefits for students, graduates, institutions and broader society alike. However, as noted earlier, the diversity of institutions and systems across Europe and also within individual countries leaves ambiguities regarding quality assurance methodologies and terminology across different cultural and national boundaries, and even between universities within the same system. There is therefore a critical responsibility to work with other systems and institutions to overcome such differences.

The development of ENQA and its sub-networks in recent years goes a long way to addressing many aspects of this European dimension for national quality assurance agencies. For example, the collective development of the standards and guidelines for quality assurance[44] by ENQA member agencies across Europe, in partnership with EUA, EURASHE and ESIB, and the acceptance of these by ministers in 2005, means that for the first time, agencies and institutions can now reference themselves explicitly

---

44. ENQA (2005), *Standards and Guidelines for Quality Assurance in the European Higher Education Area*, Helsinki.

to a set of shared quality assurance methodological principles, for both internal and external purposes.

This same drive to identify common ground on which further developments can be built in the area of quality assurance and quality improvement is also evident among higher education institutions, in the context of their various institutional or disciplinary networks. The recent projects and publications of EUA and other bodies such as Tuning are evidence of this. The same is true in the crucial area of recognition, through the ENIC/NARIC network, where the European dimension of this work has long been the central tenet.

Such initiatives can empower agencies and institutions effectively to take a wider European perspective to their own quality assurance procedures, whether through the use of common documentation, standards, guidelines, etc, through the sharing of experts and key personnel, and simply through better understanding of each other's systems and concepts. Agencies, institutions, and other bodies such as ENIC/NARICs also assume the critical responsibility of ensuring that accurate and reliable information is provided to students and their families regarding the quality of institutions and programmes, both at home and across the European higher education area.

The Nordic quality assurance network NOQA recently published a joint analysis on the ENQA standards and guidelines from a Nordic perspective,[45] taking the European dimension one stage further. One of the points noted in this analysis is that all agencies and higher education institutions operate in national contexts of system, culture and traditions, and that more precise threshold values regarding standards will be needed if we are to arrive at European consistency. The NOQA analysis points out that, as already noted, the complex terminology in such procedures means it is difficult to understand and to use in all countries and cultures. If this is true in the Nordic context, then it must be doubly true in a pan-European context.

At institutional level, leadership and governance are essential in ensuring an effective European dimension. There is considerable scope for learning in these fields across institutional and national boundaries, and many such opportunities are indeed offered by European networks and interest groups. In such ways, good practice can be spread horizontally, thus helping a coherent European higher education system to emerge, based on the development of successful and competitive individual institutions.

High levels of quality in institutions presuppose high-quality working conditions for staff, in order to attract and retain the right people. In many cases, this will depend to a large extent on improved financial resources in universities. There remains, however, an open question in many countries regarding how this can be achieved without the introduction of student fees.

---

45. Tue Vinther-Jørgensen and Signe Ploug Hansen (eds) (2007), *European Standards and Guidelines in a Nordic Perspective: Joint Nordic Project 2005-2006*; ENQA Occasional papers No. 11 (see www.enqa.eu/files/nordic_v02.pdf).

One aim of improving quality is to reduce drop-out and improve efficiency in terms of students passing their exams on time. This creates a certain pressure on students, and the introduction of student fees will further increase this. In such circumstances, the pressure on academic staff has also steadily increased to ensure that students pass exams, even if they may not be fully ready to do so. Such pressure can be seen as acting counter to other fundamental issues of quality assurance. This is one of the risks of increased marketisation of higher education, and forum participants were not aware of evidence of a quality assurance system being able to cope adequately with such a situation.

3. Evolving national quality assurance systems

Case studies from Bulgaria, Ireland and Poland were presented during the forum, illustrating the evolving nature of quality assurance systems at national level. These three cases shared a number of key features, which can be outlined as follows.

The higher education systems in these three countries have grown rapidly in recent decades, although in different ways and at slightly different times, linked to the respective social, political and economic reforms taking place in each country. An immediate and direct consequence of the rapid growth in demand for higher education has been a corresponding expansion in the number and diversity of higher education institutions. This has meant that it has also been necessary to put in place suitable quality assurance processes and practices, in order to correspond to this new reality.

The Bulgarian case showed how the state quality assurance and accreditation agency has been able, by re-focusing its work on the strategic priorities for higher education in that country, to encourage a new understanding of the importance of quality assurance in the successful implementation of those priorities. In more specific terms, some of the major successes so far have been improved student achievement rates, improved research productivity in many institutions, the sustainable development of improved curriculum and a growing internal quality culture within a wide range of institutions.

In Ireland, the expansion in higher education in the 1980s and 1990s was followed by the creation of a number of quality assurance bodies, which in recent years have begun to work closely together and to share core principles and methodologies. This closer co-operation has been helped by recent external evaluations of all the universities and of many other higher education institutions and quality assurance agencies, thus providing a series of recommendations from which the entire higher education sector can benefit. These various evaluations point to the continued importance of higher education to national development, and to the successful start that has been made by institutions and agencies in putting quality assurance systems in place, both internally and externally. However, work is still needed to ensure that the full potential of these systems is exploited to improve higher education in the coming years, notably by linking the outcomes of the quality assurance activities with broader strategic planning and reform processes at both institutional and sectoral levels. It was reported that work also remained to be done in terms of raising awareness among external stakeholders of the extent and value of the quality assurance activities already undertaken.

The Polish case demonstrated the massive expansion of the higher education system during the 1990s. According to the presentation, this expansion was not, however, accompanied by the introduction of the necessary systems to ensure satisfactory quality assurance standards or procedures. Reliable data were difficult to obtain, and there was no clear definition regarding the division of respective competences and responsibilities between higher education institutions, the ministries and other bodies. Driven by their conviction that the State Accrediting Committee was not in a position to take on the pro-active role needed to tackle this situation, a small group of universities created the University Accreditation Council, in an attempt to refocus efforts on the key issues at stake. This has resulted in a double set of procedures for the universities in question, which are still obliged to respect the programme-focused approach of the State Accrediting Committee, while in parallel developing the new institutionally focused approach. Despite this extra workload, the universities feel that their efforts will pay dividends in terms of putting in place sustainable processes based on institutional responsibility and which respect different strategic orientations and developments.

As part of these broader changes, it is interesting to note in all three cases that the main focus of the quality assurance systems being put in place, or being planned, has shifted or is expected to shift from a programme-based approach to an institutional approach. Following this methodological change, the role of the quality assurance agencies in each case has also changed, or is changing. This change in focus has been further encouraged since 2005 by the ENQA standards and guidelines document.

In each case, there has been growing awareness and acceptance of the principle that the primary responsibility for quality assurance lies within each institution, rather than in the quality assurance agency, ministry or embedded in a legislative document. This principle fits well with the need for extensive institutional autonomy and the findings of the EUA Trends IV study,[46] which showed an emerging correlation between the level of effective institutional autonomy and the existence of an internal quality culture. This is also consistent with elements from the forum case studies, which showed that a key aspect of promoting such an approach is the necessity of internal institutional integrity if an improvement-oriented quality assurance exercise is to have any lasting impact.

However, the increase in this internal institutional responsibility shown through the case studies should also be backed up by more effective external quality assurance processes, aimed at supporting internal efforts. The new dimensions to this external quality assurance process were likewise clear in the three case studies, although to different degrees. Awareness of the public responsibility for this external approach

---

46. Reichert, Sybille and Tauch, Christian, Trends IV: *European Universities Implementing Bologna,* EUA 2005, www.eua.be/eua/en/publications.jspx.

was also seen to be increasing steadily. The clearer distinction between internal and external quality assurance processes allows for greater awareness of the relative responsibilities for each of these two approaches.

A number of issues remain the subject of ongoing discussion in several of the case study countries. One of these is the question of who should pay for the various components of this quality assurance framework. Experience across many European countries has shown that putting in place and operating effective quality assurance procedures costs money, even before counting the considerable investment required if the recommendations regarding quality improvement are properly acted upon. The costs associated with operating quality assurance procedures – internal and external – can in fact become rather large, especially in systems which have a predominant focus on programme accreditation, given the large numbers of such programmes. The question therefore of who should pay – or how the costs should be shared – is a vital one.

A second such issue which has not yet been fully resolved in the countries in question is how to integrate more effectively the views of both employers and students into internal and external quality assurance activities. The roles of these stakeholders are crucial to the entire process, given current policy debates on the need for increased relevance of higher education, employability, links with society and transparency. Although these are explicitly addressed in the ENQA standards and guidelines document, considerable efforts are required in order to ensure the effective long-term engagement of these stakeholders, at institutional, agency and national levels. Regarding students, this includes fostering their representation at all levels, together with training and support so that they can assume fully their own responsibilities in this field.

4. Responsibilities of institutions

Based on the presentations and discussions in the forum, the following were identified as areas of particular responsibility for higher education institutions in the field of quality assurance.

Since the primary responsibility for quality development and quality assurance in higher education rests with the institutions themselves, as stated by ministers in their Berlin Communiqué in 2003, one of the main goals of higher education governance and management should be this continuous concern for quality.

As part of this responsibility, each higher education institution needs to make explicit its mission and strategic objectives, so that these can form the starting point for developing and assessing the quality of the institution. Different missions and objectives will require suitably relevant internal quality assurance systems. Indeed, different stages of institutional development may require different approaches and methodologies. These may change over time and will tend to shift from quantitative towards qualitative approaches as both internal and external quality assurance systems become more mature.

Since the enhancement of quality is the goal of these various approaches, an internal quality culture is needed to ensure that this is shared across the institution by all actors. Such an approach will require input and co-operation with a variety of key stakeholders, including students and external partners. The formalisation and implementation of such a quality assurance and enhancement system represents a challenge for any higher education institution, since it touches on all key aspects of the work of the institution: teaching and learning, student assessment, research, information systems, services and more.

This approach therefore also has important implications for the governance of institutions, since it calls for open systems with core quality assurance elements which different institutional players can use. Leadership, management and transparency are thus key elements of good systems, in which individual and collective efforts can develop and bear fruit, and in which the ownership of this quality culture remains embedded at grassroots levels. This quality culture should also be able to satisfy external information needs, without compromising internal integrity.

External quality assurance, carried out through mandates given by the competent public authorities, constitutes an important complement to the quality culture of higher education institutions. It is therefore also an institutional responsibility to co-operate with the agency or other body conducting the external process, so that the quality improvement benefits for the institution can be maximised. These external evaluations can have a wide variety of focuses, and the fresh perspectives which they bring need to be internalised in order to ensure that full benefits are obtained.

In working towards these general responsibilities for quality assurance, the importance of co-operation with stakeholders and partners cannot be overemphasised.

One of the purposes of quality assurance is to facilitate academic recognition for incoming and outgoing students, enhance internationalisation and promote institutional partnerships. Improved quality assurance across Europe will lead to improved recognition. Transparent quality assurance mechanisms will allow external partners, including other higher education institutions and recognition agencies, to understand and have confidence in the quality of education provision and outcomes at the institution and its respective parts. Such understanding and confidence is also contingent on adequate and understandable information in respect of the outcomes of quality reviews, which should therefore be made widely accessible.

While reports from internal and external quality assessment exercises play an important role in maintaining and improving the quality of higher education, the most critical phase in this work is the follow-up given to these reports. This follow-up should be seen as a main responsibility of the higher education institutions themselves. Quality assurance and enhancement exercises should therefore be focused on the future, should include leadership and management, and should in particular concentrate on the capacity of institutions for effective change, supported by quality culture and adequate resources.

5. Responsibilities of agencies

There has been rapid growth in the number and variety of quality assurance agencies across Europe over the last ten years. However, recent evidence, including that presented at this forum, points to the possibility that the roles of many of these agencies are converging, although this process will take a few years to complete. This search for common ground is a natural consequence of the work in progress towards establishing a coherent and effective European Higher Education Area, and has been encouraged by the agreement in 2005 of European-wide standards and guidelines for external quality assurance and the reviews of agencies. Indeed the aims of these standards and guidelines are to encourage the development of higher education institutions which themselves foster vibrant intellectual and educational achievement.

One of the most important areas of convergence is that many agencies now share the explicit objective of supporting higher education institutions in this quality enhancement process. Indeed, achieving this objective is a primary responsibility of the agencies, since without this their work will not leave lasting benefits for learners.

A second responsibility of agencies is to ensure that external quality assurance systems are fit for purpose. This follows from the need to support institutions in their own efforts, and the fact that each institution is different in terms of mission, objectives, learners, stakeholders and methods. Quality assurance agencies likewise need to recognise that different stages of institutional development may require different approaches and methodologies. The balance between methodologies may change over time and will tend to shift from quantitative towards qualitative approaches in line with the increasing maturity of the systems.

The organisation of these external quality assurance systems is a third responsibility of agencies, and an important complement to the quality culture of higher education institutions. The resources and efforts spent on external quality assurance should be commensurate with the benefits derived from it, and should be no more than necessary in order to achieve these benefits. This is particularly important when considering the range and scope of quality assurance and accreditation activities.

A number of agencies include a training and capacity-building element among their responsibilities. Since quality assurance is really about people, not systems, this aspect is important in ensuring that both the institutional actors and the external panel members are well aware of their roles, and of how they can optimise their contributions to the wider goals of quality improvement.

Monitoring, analysis and research are likewise responsibilities of many quality assurance agencies. These activities can help ensure that systems are fit for purpose, and that they evolve to follow changes in the institution and broader environment. They are also important for communicating the rationale, outcomes and long-term benefits of quality assurance to a wide variety of stakeholders, including the public authorities.

Agencies have a responsibility to ensure the responsible use of data relating to quality assurance activities. Much information is gathered during these processes, and if the process is to be honest and improvement-led, it requires that the less positive aspects of whatever is under evaluation should also be examined and discussed between internal and external experts. If this cannot take place in a climate of confidence and mutual trust, then the entire process loses its main aim. The responsible use of data is therefore an essential element, but which should not obscure the broader goals of transparency and public information.

This provision of public information is a major responsibility for agencies. Adequate and understandable information in respect of the outcomes of quality reviews should be made widely accessible. This also implies the need to develop non-specialist terminology, and to consider language issues so that important documentation is available to local actors. Given the strong links between quality assurance and the recognition of qualifications, closer co-operation between recognition and quality assurance agencies is a vital element in this field. Quality assurance is likewise an essential element for underpinning national qualifications frameworks as these are developed. Agencies need to foster broad understanding of the role of quality assurance in such frameworks.

Agencies face a growing responsibility in the area of European co-operation. Given that European countries should be seeking to place their quality assurance systems in a broader European and international context, as called for by ministers at various stages in the Bologna process, this implies increased co-operation with neighbouring systems, through regional networks, and at European level. In particular in the case of smaller higher education systems, regional co-operation could be sought in quality assurance, to ensure that available expertise and resources are put to best use.

One special area of responsibility is that of access to quality assurance for cross-border qualifications. In some cases, higher education institutions cannot currently gain access to quality assurance in the host country in which they are delivering the education. This anomaly needs to be solved in the interests of learners and wider society, and agencies have the responsibility to ensure that higher education delivered in their countries meets whatever quality assurance criteria have been set in that country.

6. Responsibilities of public authorities

The public authorities are, in the European tradition, responsible for the broad higher education framework of their country. This includes, among other essential functions, ensuring relevant and operational legislative and financing systems.

As an essential precursor to quality assurance, public authorities should also, in co-operation and consultation with higher education institutions, staff, students and other stakeholders, develop visions and goals for the higher education systems for which they are responsible, and provide the framework for their implementation.

There will inevitably be a certain diversity of implementation across European countries of the European standards and guidelines for quality assurance; this is not of concern as long as all countries are developing compatible visions and goals and are using the same reference points when putting in place internal and external quality assurance mechanisms. These common reference points are essential if we are to avoid the consequences of multiple local interpretations of these standards and guidelines. Public authorities therefore also have a responsibility to ensure that mutual trust develops across the European Higher Education Area.

Given that quality in higher education should be considered in the light of the requirements of the academic community and disciplines, as well as the broader needs and expectations of society, the public authorities also have their role to play in ensuring that due consideration is given to ethics and to opportunities for personal development. They should be in a position to satisfy themselves that higher education institutions provide equal opportunities for learners and the extent to which they stimulate innovation.

In today's context where roles in higher education are often shared between the state and its relevant agencies, the public authorities have the responsibility to ensure that these agencies fulfil their roles, and that the judgment of an independent agency prevails over local political decisions. This responsibility also extends to ensuring that there is policy coherence across all relevant agencies and other public bodies, and that over-regulation is avoided.

Public authorities should likewise ensure that higher education institutions are fulfilling their roles in the field of quality assurance. This implies that they encourage the monitoring of quality assurance and quality enhancement activities within institutions. Such encouragement can be offered in many ways, notably through the use of financial and other incentives. Rewarding quality enhancement has become a key mechanism of public authorities in a number of European countries in their efforts to promote quality assurance.

As custodians of the public good, authorities should ensure that adequate, understandable and pertinent public information in respect of the outcomes of quality reviews is made widely accessible, particularly to key stakeholders. This information should relate not only to the providers of higher education but also to the quality assurance agencies and their activities. The proposed European register of quality assurance agencies therefore takes on extra importance in terms of ensuring broad understanding and acceptance of the work of these agencies.

Given that the development and maintenance of good-quality higher education and research are contingent on attractive working conditions for staff and students, and that quality assurance activities cost money, a major responsibility of the public authorities is to ensure that sufficient funding is available for these. Of particular importance is the need to ensure funding is available for follow-up activities and working towards improvements identified during the evaluation process. The tradition in Europe has been that the costs of quality assurance have been covered by national systems of higher education.

7. Legitimacy

The definition, development and assessment of quality are complementary aspects of the quest for quality in higher education and research. Quality assurance is therefore linked to an ongoing debate on the goals of higher education and research, as well as to continuous work to improve the ability of institutions, staff and students to meet these goals.

The legitimacy of quality assurance in higher education therefore depends not only on the legal status of institutions or procedures, but on the transparency and coherence of this debate and ongoing work throughout Europe. These are essential elements in ensuring the credibility of both the providers and the external agencies.

The basic credibility for this broader European quality assurance context now rests on the Bologna process, and on the commitment of ministers, higher education institutions, staff, students and stakeholders to work towards the Bologna goals.

This European dimension has added an extra layer of legitimacy to quality assurance processes. Since they are now based on Bologna process principles, building on trust between institutions, agencies, and public authorities, it is hoped that all key actors and stakeholders should now be in a position to feel ownership of both the methods and results.

This legitimacy depends on a number of concepts which are key to the success of the broader Bologna process. These include transparency, participation and communication. The new and growing awareness across Europe of the importance of seeing quality assurance as an improvement-oriented process, not as a control mechanism, is certainly helping add to this sense of legitimacy.

Quality assurance is continuously moving, and great strides have been made in many respects since the start of the Bologna process. The time element in this work is important, since not all can be achieved at once, and balanced approaches, grounded in the core values of higher education and research, are needed to ensure that the legitimacy of quality assurance continues to grow among all actors and stakeholders. This added sense of legitimacy will also add to the real value of the work itself, not just to its effectiveness but also to the degree of ownership and responsibility by each of the key actors in the process – institutions, agencies and public authorities.

Conclusions and recommendations

The Council of Europe Higher Education Forum on The Legitimacy of Quality Assurance in Higher Education: the Role of Public Authorities and Institutions, held in Strasbourg on 19-20 September 2006 with the co-operation of ENQA and the EUA, focused on the relationship between quality assurance, the public responsibility for higher education and research, and higher education governance.

The forum took as its starting point the premise that striving to achieve high quality underlies higher education and research, and that achievement of quality is a joint responsibility of all partners in higher education. Institutions, staff and students as well as public authorities should continue to see quality improvement as an essential goal of their learning, teaching and research.

Quality in higher education should be considered in the light of the requirements of the academic community and disciplines as well as the broader needs and expectations of society, of which higher education and research are a part. This should include considerations of ethics and opportunities for personal development as well as of the extent to which institutions provide equal opportunities for learners and the extent to which they stimulate innovation.

Public authorities should, in co-operation and consultation with higher education institutions, staff, students and other stakeholders, develop visions and goals for the higher education systems for which they are responsible and provide the framework for their implementation. They should seek to develop mutual trust within the European Higher Education Area.

Higher education institutions should make explicit their mission and aims, which should then form the basis for the development and assessment of the quality of the institution.

The definition, development and assessment of quality are complementary aspects of the quest for quality in higher education and research. Quality assurance, therefore, is linked to an ongoing debate on the goals of higher education and research as well as continuous work to improve the ability of institutions, staff and students to meet those goals.

Public authorities as well as institutions and quality assurance agencies should recognise that different stages of development of institutions and higher education systems may require different approaches and methodologies. These may include the use of quantitative and qualitative indicators and criteria, which may vary according to the stage of development of the system. The balance between methodologies may change over time and will tend to shift from quantitative towards qualitative approaches in line with the increasing maturity of the systems.

The development and maintenance of good-quality higher education and research are contingent on attractive working conditions for staff and students as well as on the framework laid down by public authorities.

The forum expressed support for the standards and guidelines for quality assurance in the European Higher Education Area adopted by ministers in Bergen in May 2005.

Since, as stated by ministers in their Berlin Communiqué, the main responsibility for quality development and quality assurance in higher education rests with the institutions, higher education governance and management must have the continuous development of quality as one of its main goals. Public authorities should encourage and ensure monitoring of quality assurance and quality enhancement activities.

Quality enhancement should be a continuous concern of, and mobilise, higher education institutions and all their members individually. Institutions should also seek input from and co-operation with external stakeholders.

External quality assurance, carried out through mandates given by competent public authorities, constitutes an important complement to the quality culture of higher education institutions. The resources and efforts spent on external quality assurance should be commensurate with the benefits derived from it and should be no more than necessary to achieve these benefits. This is particularly important when considering the range and scope of quality assurance and accreditation activities.

While reports from internal and external quality assessment exercises play an important role in maintaining and improving the quality of higher education, the most critical phase in this work is the follow-up given to these reports, which should be seen as a main responsibility of the higher education institutions themselves. Quality assurance and enhancement exercises should therefore be focused on the future, should include leadership and management, and should in particular concentrate on the capacity of institutions for effective change, supported by quality culture and adequate resources.

All European countries should be seeking to place their systems in a broader European and international context. In particular in the case of smaller higher education systems, regional co-operation could be sought in quality assurance.

Adequate and understandable information in respect of the outcomes of quality reviews should be made widely accessible.

Quality assurance should contribute to enhancing fair recognition of qualifications across the European Higher Education Area, which requires adequate information on the quality of education provision and outcomes as well as closer co-operation between recognition and quality assurance agencies.

The Council of Europe and its Steering Committee for Higher Education and Research (CDESR) should use its position as a pan-European platform anchored in an organisation of values to ensure that the core values of universities are embedded in the European Higher Education Area and help find adequate ways to nurture these as our societies change.

List of contributors

Alberto Amaral

Alberto Amaral is professor at the University of Porto and director of CIPES. He was a former rector of the University of Porto (1986-98). He is chair of the Board of CHER, life member of IAUP, and a member of EAIR, IMHE and SCUP. Recent publications include papers in *Quality Assurance in Education, Higher Education Quarterly, Higher Education Policy, Higher Education in Europe, European Journal of Education, Higher Education, Tertiary Education Management, Higher Education Management and Policy, Quality in Higher Education* and *Planning for Higher Education*. He is a member of the editorial board of *Quality Assurance in Education* and of the Springer book series, Higher Education Dynamics. He is editor and co-editor of several books, including *Governing Higher Education: National Perspectives on Institutional Governance* (2002), *The Higher Education Managerial Revolution?* (2003), *Markets in Higher Education: Rhetoric or Reality?* (2004) and *Reform and Change in Higher Education: Analysing Policy Implementation* (2005).

Fergal Costello

Fergal Costello worked from 1995 to 1998 in the Central Policy Unit of the Department of Education and Science in Ireland; from 1998 to 1999 in the Public Expenditure Division of the Department of Finance; from 1999 to 2001 in the Policy Unit of the Department of Education and Science.

In 2001 Fergal joined the Higher Education Authority (HEA) as Head of Policy and Planning where he was involved in many HEA projects including:

- Admission to Medical Education – implementation of a new and revised entry mechanism to medical school for graduates and undergraduates;
- the preparation of the HEA submission to the OECD review team on Irish higher education, 2004;
- the preparation of the HEA/Forfas report on attracting retaining researchers to Ireland 2003;
- the implementation of the HEA's statutory function on review of equality policies in the universities 2003-04.

In March 2006 he became the head of the Institutes of Technology Section, a new section which will manage the transition of the Institute of Technology sector under the remit of the HEA. The principal focus of the section will relate to the management of the funding allocation and the development a new funding system and wider policy issues relating to the development of the sector.

Fergal is also an adviser to the Expert Group on Future Skills Needs.

Patricia Georgieva

Patricia Georgieva graduated in Education Studies at Sofia University "St Kliment Ohridski", Faculty of Philosophy, in 1979. In 1988 she earned a doctor's degree in Education. In 2003 she became a habilitated research fellow in Education.

Mrs Georgieva specialised in the field of quality improvement in higher education at the London Institute of Education, London University, in 1996-97.

She was a research fellow at the Institute for Higher Education Research between 1982 and 1990 and then at the National Institute of Education. From 1998 to 2002 she was head of the Centre for Higher Education Research. In this position she contributed to the comprehensive study of higher education in Bulgaria in the UNESCO-CEPES Monographs on Higher Education series, which reflects the profound changes that have been occurring in Bulgaria in the context of transition that began in 1989.

Since October, 2002 she has been chief executive officer of the National Evaluation and Accreditation Agency. Her recent professional experience includes drafting short- and medium-term education strategies, and drafting higher education legislation with specific reference to quality assurance, evaluation and accreditation, policy development and research planning.

Jürgen Kohler

Jürgen Kohler is professor of private law and private litigation at Greifswald University, Germany. He was one of the founders of the re-established faculty of law and business management of Greifswald University after German reunification in 1990. He was rector of Greifswald University between 1994 and 2000. Since then he has represented the German institutions of higher education in the CDESR of the Council of Europe and has been a member of its bureau since 2002. He is active in the Institutional Evaluation Programme of the European University Association, serving in peer-based evaluations across Europe and in its steering committee. He chairs the German Accreditation Council.

Ossi V Lindqvist

Ossi V. Lindqvist was elected chairman of the Finnish Higher Education Evaluation Council from 2000 to 2003, and again for a second term from 2004 to 2007. Before retiring in 2004, he served as professor and director at the Institute of Applied Biotechnology at the University of Kuopio, Finland. From 1990 to 1998, he served as Rector of the university. He has also served as chairman of the Finnish University Rectors' Council from 1993 to 1997, and was a member of the National Council for Science and Technology Policy from 1996 to 1999. He is also a lifetime foreign member of the Royal Swedish Academy of Agriculture and Forestry. He was professor at the University of Dayton, Ohio, USA from 1970 to 1972. Dr Lindqvist holds a PhD from the University of Turku, Finland.

Dr Lindqvist has served as evaluator or in an advisory role for several dozen European, and especially eastern European universities. He has served as consultant to several international organisations, including UNESCO, in matters related to higher education. His current special activity and expertise covers management and technology transfer issues in higher education at large, as well as development of quality assurance systems in higher education institutions.

Lewis Purser

Lewis Purser is assistant director (academic affairs) at the Irish Universities Association. From 1998 to 2005 he was programme manager at the European University Association. A graduate of Trinity College Dublin and of the Graduate Institute of Development Studies at the University of Geneva, he worked from 1989 to 1998 with various higher education institutions in Hungary, Romania and Bosnia-Herzegovina, and with several United Nations agencies in educational, health and social fields. In addition to his work at IUA, Lewis continues his links with EUA as an editor of the EUA Bologna Handbook, as a researcher on the EUA Trends project monitoring the implementation of the Bologna process across Europe, and as a member of EUA institutional evaluation teams.

Andrejs Rauhvargers

Professor Andrejs Rauhvargers is Secretary General of the Latvian Rectors' Conference. He is the President of the Committee of the Lisbon Recognition Convention and bureau member of Council of Europe's Higher Education and Research Committee. He currently chairs the working group that is carrying out the Bologna process stocktaking for the 2007 London ministerial conference.

Norman Sharp

As Director of QAA Scotland, Norman is responsible for the development and implementation of QAA's policy and practice in Scotland. In this context he played a major role in the development and implementation of the Scottish Quality Enhancement Framework – a framework which binds quality assurance and enhancement closely together involving extensive student participation.

Originally an academic economist, Norman's interest in quality assurance and enhancement was stimulated by his roles in Glasgow Caledonian University and the Open University in curriculum development and course management for "traditional" higher education students and also in the context of wider patterns of provision including part-time and work-based provision. Immediately prior to taking up his current appointment, Norman was an Assistant Director in the Higher Education Quality Council.

Norman has had extensive international involvement in quality matters including work in South Africa, Ireland, Namibia, Luxembourg, Serbia and Albania. He has also been a consultant on quality matters to a range of employers and professional and statutory bodies. In 2006, he was the Chairman of NHS Quality Improvement Scotland, the body responsible for the assurance and enhancement of provision in the National Health Service in Scotland.

Norman was awarded the OBE by HM Queen Elizabeth II in the 2006 New Year's Honours List for services to higher education.

Luc Weber

Educated in the fields of economics and political science, Luc Weber has been Professor of Public Economics at the University of Geneva since 1975. As an economist, he serves as an adviser to Switzerland's federal government, as well as to cantonal governments, and has been a member of the Swiss Council of Economic Advisers for three years. Since 1982, Professor Weber has been deeply involved in university management and higher education policy, first as vice-rector, then as rector of the University of Geneva, as well as Chairman and, subsequently, Consul for international affairs of the Swiss Rectors' Conference. He is also the co-founder, with Werner Hirsch, of the Glion Colloquium and a funding Board Member of the European University Association (EUA). At present he is chair of the Steering Committee for Higher Education and Research of the Council of Europe and vice-president of the International Association of Universities (IAU). He was recently awarded an honorary degree by the Catholic University of Louvain-la-Neuve for his contribution to higher education.

Peter Williams

Peter Williams is a graduate in English from the University of Exeter. Following a brief spell as a management trainee with the British Printing Corporation, and three years in the Registry of the University of Surrey, he moved in 1974 to the University of Leicester, where he was in charge of the Higher Degrees Office. In 1978 he was promoted to Assistant Registrar in the Medical School, becoming Secretary of the School in 1982. In 1984 he was appointed Deputy Secretary of the British Academy. In 1990 Peter was appointed as the first (and only) Director of the CVCP Academic Audit Unit (AAU), and between 1992 and 1997 was the Director of the Quality Assurance Group of the Higher Education Quality Council (HEQC), which took over the responsibilities of the AAU. In August 1997 Peter became the Director of Institutional Review in the Quality Assurance Agency for Higher Education (QAA), which was formed by a merger of HEQC and the quality assessment divisions of the UK's higher education funding councils. In August 2001 he additionally took on the role of Acting Chief Executive. In March 2002 he was appointed Chief Executive.

In addition to his work in the UK, Peter has lectured and made presentations in many other countries and has participated in a number of international quality assurance projects in Argentina, Australia, Azerbaijan, India, New Zealand, Poland, Romania, Sweden and the USA. In September 2005 he was elected President of the European Association for Quality Assurance in Higher Education (ENQA) and represents ENQA on the Bologna Follow-Up Group (BFUG).

Appendix

European quality assurance standards, adopted by the Ministers of Education of the Bologna Process in May 2005

The Bergen Conference of European Ministers responsible for Higher Education (19-20 May 2005) adopted standards and guidelines for quality assurance in the European Higher Education Area. The standards are given here for easy reference. The complete set of standards and guidelines are given in the ENQA report *Standards and Guidelines for Quality Assurance in the European Higher Education Area.*

A. European standards for internal quality assurance within higher education institutions

1. Policy and procedures for quality assurance

Institutions should have a policy and associated procedures for the assurance of the quality and standards of their programmes and awards. They should also commit themselves explicitly to the development of a culture which recognises the importance of quality, and quality assurance, in their work. To achieve this, institutions should develop and implement a strategy for the continuous enhancement of quality. The strategy, policy and procedures should have a formal status and be publicly available. They should also include a role for students and other stakeholders.

2. Approval, monitoring and periodic review of programmes and awards

Institutions should have formal mechanisms for the approval, periodic review and monitoring of their programmes and awards.

3. Assessment of students

Students should be assessed using published criteria, regulations and procedures which are applied consistently.

4. Quality assurance of teaching staff

Institutions should have ways of satisfying themselves that staff involved in the teaching of students are qualified and competent with regard to teaching. The methods and procedures for ensuring that this is the case should be available to those undertaking external reviews, and commented upon in reports.

5. Learning resources and student support

Institutions should ensure that the resources available for the support of student learning are adequate and appropriate for each programme offered.

6. Information systems

Institutions should ensure that they collect, analyse and use relevant information for the effective management of their programmes of study and other activities.

7. Public information

Institutions should regularly publish up-to-date, impartial and objective information, both quantitative and qualitative, about the programmes and awards they are offering.

B. European standards for the external quality assurance of higher education

1. Use of internal quality assurance procedures

External quality assurance procedures should take into account the effectiveness of the internal quality assurance processes described in Part A above.

2. Development of external quality assurance processes

The aims and objectives of quality assurance processes should be determined before the processes themselves are developed, by all those responsible (including higher education institutions) and should be published with a description of the procedures to be used.

3. Criteria for decisions

Any formal decisions made as a result of an external quality assurance activity should be based on explicit published criteria that are applied consistently.

4. Processes fit for purpose

All external quality assurance processes should be designed specifically to ensure their fitness to achieve the aims and objectives set for them.

5. Reporting

Reports should be published and should be written in a style which is clear and readily accessible to their intended readership. Any decisions, commendations or recommendations contained in reports should be easy for a reader to find.

6. Follow-up procedures

Quality assurance processes which contain recommendations for action or which require a subsequent action plan, should have a predetermined follow-up procedure which is implemented consistently.

7. Periodic reviews

External quality assurance of institutions and/or programmes should be undertaken on a cyclical basis. The length of the cycle and the review procedures to be used should be clearly defined and published in advance.

8. System-wide analyses

Quality assurance agencies should produce from time to time summary reports describing and analysing the general findings of their reviews, evaluations, assessments etc.

C. European standards for external quality assurance agencies

1. Use of external quality assurance procedures for higher education

The external quality assurance of agencies should take into account the presence and effectiveness of the external quality assurance processes described in Part B above.

2. Official status

Agencies should be formally recognised by competent public authorities in the European Higher Education Area as agencies with responsibilities for external quality assurance and should have an established legal basis. They should comply with any requirements of the legislative jurisdictions within which they operate.

3. Activities

Agencies should undertake external quality assurance activities (at institutional or programme level) on a regular basis.

4. Resources

Agencies should have adequate and proportional resources, both human and financial, to enable them to organise and run their external quality assurance process(es) in an effective and efficient manner, with appropriate provision for the development of their processes and procedures.

5. Mission statement

Agencies should have clear and explicit goals and objectives for their work, contained in a publicly available statement.

6. Independence

Agencies should be independent to the extent both that they have autonomous responsibility for their operations and that the conclusions and recommendations made in their reports cannot be influenced by third parties such as higher education institutions, ministries or other stakeholders.

7. External quality assurance criteria and processes used by the agencies

The processes, criteria and procedures used by agencies should be pre-defined and publicly available. These processes will normally be expected to include:

1. a self-assessment or equivalent procedure by the subject of the quality assurance process;

2. an external assessment by a group of experts, including, as appropriate, (a) student member(s), and site visits as decided by the agency;

3. publication of a report, including any decisions, recommendations or other formal outcomes;

4. a follow-up procedure to review actions taken by the subject of the quality assurance process in the light of any recommendations contained in the report.

8. Accountability procedures

Agencies should have in place procedures for their own accountability.

Sales agents for publications of the Council of Europe
Agents de vente des publications du Conseil de l'Europe

BELGIUM/BELGIQUE
La Librairie Européenne -
The European Bookshop
Rue de l'Orme, 1
B-1040 BRUXELLES
Tel.: +32 (0)2 231 04 35
Fax: +32 (0)2 735 08 60
E-mail: order@libeurop.be
http://www.libeurop.be

Jean De Lannoy
Avenue du Roi 202 Koningslaan
B-1190 BRUXELLES
Tel.: +32 (0)2 538 43 08
Fax: +32 (0)2 538 08 41
E-mail: jean.de.lannoy@dl-servi.com
http://www.jean-de-lannoy.be

CANADA
Renouf Publishing Co. Ltd.
1-5369 Canotek Road
OTTAWA, Ontario K1J 9J3, Canada
Tel.: +1 613 745 2665
Fax: +1 613 745 7660
Toll-Free Tel.: (866) 767-6766
E-mail: order.dept@renoufbooks.com
http://www.renoufbooks.com

CZECH REPUBLIC/
RÉPUBLIQUE TCHÈQUE
Suweco CZ, s.r.o.
Klecakova 347
CZ-180 21 PRAHA 9
Tel.: +420 2 424 59 204
Fax: +420 2 848 21 646
E-mail: import@suweco.cz
http://www.suweco.cz

DENMARK/DANEMARK
GAD
Vimmelskaftet 32
DK-1161 KØBENHAVN K
Tel.: +45 77 66 60 00
Fax: +45 77 66 60 01
E-mail: gad@gad.dk
http://www.gad.dk

FINLAND/FINLANDE
Akateeminen Kirjakauppa
PO Box 128
Keskuskatu 1
FIN-00100 HELSINKI
Tel.: +358 (0)9 121 4430
Fax: +358 (0)9 121 4242
E-mail: akatilaus@akateeminen.com
http://www.akateeminen.com

FRANCE
La Documentation française
(diffusion/distribution France entière)
124, rue Henri Barbusse
F-93308 AUBERVILLIERS CEDEX
Tél.: +33 (0)1 40 15 70 00
Fax: +33 (0)1 40 15 68 00
E-mail: commande@ladocumentationfrancaise.fr
http://www.ladocumentationfrancaise.fr

Librairie Kléber
1 rue des Francs Bourgeois
F-67000 STRASBOURG
Tel.: +33 (0)3 88 15 78 88
Fax: +33 (0)3 88 15 78 80
E-mail: francois.wolfermann@librairie-kleber.fr
http://www.librairie-kleber.com

GERMANY/ALLEMAGNE
AUSTRIA/AUTRICHE
UNO Verlag GmbH
August-Bebel-Allee 6
D-53175 BONN
Tel.: +49 (0)228 94 90 20
Fax: +49 (0)228 94 90 222
E-mail: bestellung@uno-verlag.de
http://www.uno-verlag.de

GREECE/GRÈCE
Librairie Kauffmann s.a.
Stadiou 28
GR-105 64 ATHINAI
Tel.: +30 210 32 55 321
Fax.: +30 210 32 30 320
E-mail: ord@otenet.gr
http://www.kauffmann.gr

HUNGARY/HONGRIE
Euro Info Service kft.
1137 Bp. Szent István krt. 12.
H-1137 BUDAPEST
Tel.: +36 (06)1 329 2170
Fax: +36 (06)1 349 2053
E-mail: euroinfo@euroinfo.hu
http://www.euroinfo.hu

ITALY/ITALIE
Licosa SpA
Via Duca di Calabria, 1/1
I-50125 FIRENZE
Tel.: +39 0556 483215
Fax: +39 0556 41257
E-mail: licosa@licosa.com
http://www.licosa.com

MEXICO/MEXIQUE
Mundi-Prensa México, S.A. De C.V.
Río Pánuco, 141 Delegacíon Cuauhtémoc
06500 MÉXICO, D.F.
Tel.: +52 (01)55 55 33 56 58
Fax: +52 (01)55 55 14 67 99
E-mail: mundiprensa@mundiprensa.com.mx
http://www.mundiprensa.com.mx

NETHERLANDS/PAYS-BAS
De Lindeboom Internationale Publicaties b.v.
M.A. de Ruyterstraat 20 A
NL-7482 BZ HAAKSBERGEN
Tel.: +31 (0)53 5740004
Fax: +31 (0)53 5729296
E-mail: books@delindeboom.com
http://www.delindeboom.com

NORWAY/NORVÈGE
Akademika
Postboks 84 Blindern
N-0314 OSLO
Tel.: +47 2 218 8100
Fax: +47 2 218 8103
E-mail: support@akademika.no
http://www.akademika.no

POLAND/POLOGNE
Ars Polona JSC
25 Obroncow Street
PL-03-933 WARSZAWA
Tel.: +48 (0)22 509 86 00
Fax: +48 (0)22 509 86 10
E-mail: arspolona@arspolona.com.pl
http://www.arspolona.com.pl

PORTUGAL
Livraria Portugal
(Dias & Andrade, Lda.)
Rua do Carmo, 70
P-1200-094 LISBOA
Tel.: +351 21 347 42 82 / 85
Fax: +351 21 347 02 64
E-mail: info@livrariaportugal.pt
http://www.livrariaportugal.pt

RUSSIAN FEDERATION/
FÉDÉRATION DE RUSSIE
Ves Mir
9a, Kolpacnhyi per.
RU-101000 MOSCOW
Tel.: +7 (8)495 623 6839
Fax: +7 (8)495 625 4269
E-mail: orders@vesmirbooks.ru
http://www.vesmirbooks.ru

SPAIN/ESPAGNE
Mundi-Prensa Libros, s.a.
Castelló, 37
E-28001 MADRID
Tel.: +34 914 36 37 00
Fax: +34 915 75 39 98
E-mail: libreria@mundiprensa.es
http://www.mundiprensa.com

SWITZERLAND/SUISSE
Van Diermen Editions – ADECO
Chemin du Lacuez 41
CH-1807 BLONAY
Tel.: +41 (0)21 943 26 73
Fax: +41 (0)21 943 36 05
E-mail: info@adeco.org
http://www.adeco.org

UNITED KINGDOM/ROYAUME-UNI
The Stationery Office Ltd
PO Box 29
GB-NORWICH NR3 1GN
Tel.: +44 (0)870 600 5522
Fax: +44 (0)870 600 5533
E-mail: book.enquiries@tso.co.uk
http://www.tsoshop.co.uk

UNITED STATES and CANADA/
ÉTATS-UNIS et CANADA
Manhattan Publishing Company
468 Albany Post Road
CROTTON-ON-HUDSON, NY 10520, USA
Tel.: +1 914 271 5194
Fax: +1 914 271 5856
E-mail: Info@manhattanpublishing.com
http://www.manhattanpublishing.com

Council of Europe Publishing/Editions du Conseil de l'Europe
F-67075 Strasbourg Cedex
Tel.: +33 (0)3 88 41 25 81 – Fax: +33 (0)3 88 41 39 10 – E-mail: publishing@coe.int – Website: http://book.coe.int